Handcrafted

A Woodworker's Story

Clint Harp

TOUCHSTONE

New York London Toronto Sydney New Delhi

Touchstone
An Imprint of Simon & Schuster, Inc.
1230 Avenue of the Americas
New York, NY 10020

Some names and identifying characteristics have been changed.

First Touchstone hardcover edition September 2018

TOUCHSTONE and colophon are registered trademarks of Simon & Schuster, Inc.

For information about special discounts for bulk purchases, please contact Simon & Schuster Special Sales at 1-866-506-1949 or business@simonandschuster.com.

The Simon & Schuster Speakers Bureau can bring authors to your live event. For more information or to book an event, contact the Simon & Schuster Speakers Bureau at 1-866-248-3049 or visit our website at www.simonspeakers.com.

Illustrations by Darrah Gooden
Interior design by Kyle Kabel

Manufactured in the United States of America

10   9   8   7   6   5   4   3   2   1

Library of Congress Cataloging-in-Publication Data
Names: Harp, Clint, author.
Title: Handcrafted / by Clint Harp.
Description: New York : Touchstone, [2018]
Identifiers: LCCN 2018018648| ISBN 9781501188985 (hardcover) | ISBN
    9781501188992 (pbk.)
Subjects: LCSH: Harp, Clint. | Cabinetmakers—United States—Biography. |
    Furniture making—Anecdotes.
Classification: LCC TT140.H37 A3 2018 | DDC 684.1/04092 [B] —dc23
LC record available at https://lccn.loc.gov/2018018648

ISBN 978-1-5011-8898-5
ISBN 978-1-5011-8900-5 (ebook)

This book is dedicated to my wife, Kelly,
and to my three children Hudson, Holland, and Camille.
Every path I've ever journeyed has led me to you.
Each road came with its own set of difficulties and obstacles,
and I would travel them all a million times to end up by your side.

A man who works with his hands is a laborer.

A man who works with his hands and his brain is a craftsman.

But a man who works with his hands and his brain and his heart is an artist.

—Louis Nizer, lawyer, writer, and painter

Contents

CONTENTS

PART THREE: JOURNEYMAN

Handcrafted

A Seed Is Planted

Building a table, for me, starts with a vision—a seed of an idea. Whether I'm out for a morning run, working in my shop, talking with my wife, or playing with my kids, somewhere I'm sparked with an idea. This dream may revolve around a need, a specific design, or the very real thought of friends and family sitting around the table I feel compelled to build. To be inspired by a vision and then be able to create a physical representation of that vision is a gift I'll never take for granted.

In elementary school, my teacher took us outside and asked us all to find a tree. Once we found one, she said, that tree would be ours; we could adopt it as our very own. Although I was born in Atlanta, at that time I lived in Asheville, North Carolina, where beautiful trees were abundant. I was six years old and in the first grade. I found my tree and sat down at its base. My classmates and I just sat there by our trees, quietly getting acquainted with our tall new friends. For all I know, my teacher was at the end of her rope that day, and she came up with this activity as a way to just keep us quiet for a few minutes. I don't know her reasons and never will, but it doesn't matter. For me, the experience was magical. That tree was mine and I loved it. I scratched in the dirt at its base, and then dug a little deeper. I kept digging until I found a little rock. I lifted it from the ground and thought that maybe, just maybe, I was the only one to ever touch that rock—it had come from the hand of its creator straight to mine, with no one in between. That day, my heart cracked open to life's mysterious possibilities.

Decades later, when I quit my job to pursue a passion to build furniture, in my mind I was once again sitting at the base of that tree. Hidden deep in my heart was an old wooden door, leading to a room full of dreams. For many reasons—not the least of which were society's ideas about what it means to "grow up" and "get serious" and "be a good provider"—I had closed that door years before. But now it had been flung open. I had walked back into a world where anything was possible. For you, that door might have opened onto a classroom, a farm, a playing field, a church sanctuary, a medical school, an auto repair shop, an art studio. For me, that door opened onto a woodshop—my garage, to be exact. Inside that sweltering space was a universe bigger than any I'd ever imagined, one that I had discovered only because I'd found the courage to embrace the journey that had been calling to me for some time.

I have a story. So do you. And as we stumble along, trying to follow our dreams and find our way, we're filling the pages of a giant book called *life*. All those who came before us, the men and women whose names we don't always know but who helped lay the path we now travel, had their stories as well. And many more will come after us, making their own contributions and building on what we've left behind.

Take those workers who built the awe-inspiring Notre-Dame Cathedral in Paris: the first time I stared up at this French Gothic masterpiece, with its glorious stained-glass windows and magnificent sculptures, I was blown away. How, without electricity, could mere mortals have built such a place? As I wandered through the sanctuary, I began to understand that the workers' stories were in the very walls, and that all artisans, ancient or modern, leave us their art wrapped in a mystery we get to explore. If we tune into it, we can find inspiration in every turn of wood or note of music, every stroke of the pen or daub of paint. It's right there, waiting for us.

Countless musicians, painters, writers, and sculptors have shaped my own work, and I'll forever wish that I could sit and have a conversation with just a few of them over a beer and a table full of food. But even without knowing the details of the sweat and angst they poured into their artistry, I'm still inspired to do as they did, to embrace both possibilities and impossibilities, to dare to walk into my woodshop every day and work with my chosen tools.

I've learned that handcrafting a life is a lot like woodwork, really. You know you want to create something beautiful, a piece that will last. So you take some lumber, make your first rough cut, and go from there. And the process that carries you from the first rough cut to the last finishing coat—that's what makes the masterpiece.

This book is the story of the path I've taken: how I got here, where I've been, and where I think I'm going. In sharing it, I'm also telling the stories of those who believed in me and pushed me along: all those who brought me into this world and raised me to be the man I am, and of course the woman who became my wife, Kelly, who dreamed this journey with me and dared to embark upon it along with our three children.

This is not a self-help book, but it is, in part, a book about how I helped myself. It's not a how-to manual, but you'll definitely learn how I've attempted to blaze a trail for myself. It doesn't have all the answers, but hopefully it shows how I've found a few of my own. As you read, I hope you'll find yourself in my story, just as

I'd likely find myself in yours. At a time in our world when too much focus has been given to what divides us, we'll always have a few incredibly important things in common: our pilgrimage through life. The company of other travelers. And those magical, sky-opening moments like the one I experienced at the base of an old tree.

PART ONE

LABORER

You belong among the wildflowers.

—Tom Petty, singer/songwriter

CHAPTER 1

Milled

When the wood is lying in piles on the floor, all out of order and in every shape and size, I'm no longer thinking about the finished product. Rather, I'm turning my full attention to creating, one board at a time. The entire process is a matter of trial and error. I might imagine it one way, discover that it doesn't look great, and then reimagine it and start again. As it goes with furniture, so it goes with life: it's a process, and there's no magic manual, no ironclad set of rules for every single situation. Sometimes you just gather up the broken pieces from the splinters and the sawdust and you improvise.

Just off the main highway that runs through Waco, Texas, sits a pink house—one built in that kind of Southwestern adobe style you might find in Arizona or Nevada. Back when it was constructed in the late 1920s, it might have been a gem of a property. But years of neglect, harsh weather, and the unrelenting Texas sun had worn it down so that now it just looked rickety. That didn't matter to my wife, Kelly. She loved it right away.

We first saw the place a few weeks after we moved with our two children to Waco to begin a new chapter in our lives. "That's a great house," Kelly said, pointing, as we drove past one afternoon. I slowed down a bit and then pulled over so we could get a closer look.

"Really?" I said, eyeing the crumbling facade and the uncut grass of the yard. "It's in pretty bad shape."

"I know," Kelly said, "but we could renovate it."

"With what money?" I said dubiously.

"You never know . . . it doesn't hurt to dream." said Kelly to the guy who dreamed all the time but whose dreams were now starting to fade.

Dreaming is what had led us to Waco. In December 2011, we'd moved back to our old college town so that Kelly could pursue a graduate degree in American studies at Baylor University, our alma mater. Waco held fond memories for us; it was the place where we'd met as students, begun dating, and eventually gotten engaged. Our dream this time around was for Kelly to go back to school while we also worked to get our new business, Harp Design Co., off the ground. My task was to find a shop, out of which I would build handcrafted furniture that we would then sell to anyone who would give us a chance. It was a desire I'd had ever since I was a boy sitting around the nine-foot yellow pine table my grandfather crafted with his own hands. That stained, scarred, timeworn piece had become a family heirloom, and the memory of it made me want to build lasting pieces of my own. Problem was, starting a carpentry business takes money, or so I thought, and Kelly and I had none.

Four years earlier in Houston, things had been different. I'd landed a job in medical sales with a wonderful company and was making more money than I'd ever seen. I was also brutally unhappy. I mean, cry me a river, right? A cushy paycheck. A house and two cars. A neighborhood pool. A great schedule. From the outside, our life appeared enviable, and in many ways, it was, but every Monday when I dragged myself to work, I felt as if I were drowning. I soldiered forward, mostly out of a desire to be a strong provider.

Yet as one year stretched into four and I grew more miserable by the minute, it became clear that I was living someone else's version of the Good Life.

So I quit. In May 2011, Kelly and I traded an annual salary that dwarfed any I'd ever imagined for myself so that I could jump in my garage and build furniture and we could start a company together. And we did it with just enough money to last us for six to eight months if I sold nothing. Of course, in my mind, we were going to sell a bunch of pieces right away, which definitely didn't happen. In fact, even after we blew through our piggy bank, we were still struggling to imagine what our business would even look like.

A couple of months before our well ran dry, Kelly announced, "I'd like to go back and get my master's." Now, I know what you're thinking, because it's exactly what I was thinking: *Are you kidding? Graduate school? We hardly have money for groceries.* Yet as overextended as we were, some part of me—the part that had walked away from the soul-crushing effort of hanging on to a job I knew wasn't for me—was crazy enough to believe that we could make it work. A few months later, we'd receive the news that not only had Baylor accepted her, the program also gave her a full scholarship. That pointed the way to our next stop. We were heading to Waco.

One weekend early in 2012, not long after we'd relocated and run across the pink house, some friends of Kelly's from undergrad, James and Adrianna, invited us to dinner. When you're as penniless as we were, being invited to eat anywhere is the best news ever. Over pizza, James asked why we'd moved back to Waco. Kelly's answer was straightforward. Mine was less so.

"I'm trying to build furniture for a living," I told him.

"Oh, where's your shop?" he asked.

Long pause. "Well, I don't have one yet," I said.

"So what are you doing for work in the meantime?"

Awkward silence. "Well, I'm volunteering right now, but I'm on the lookout for a shop."

Mercifully, the conversation moved on. But as we were saying our good-byes after dinner, James pulled me aside.

"You should call a friend of mine," he suggested. He explained that his pal Chip had a lot of connections around town and might be able to help me locate a shop. He gave me Chip's number, and a few days later, I called.

There's a *Seinfeld* episode titled "The Phone Message." In it, George Costanza, the fumbling, anxious buddy of Jerry Seinfeld, goes on a date. Things turn out well except for the fact that, at the end of the evening, he misses an obvious clue to extend the date, which leaves him feeling like an idiot. The next day, George hasn't heard from the woman, so he calls her. The message is a dumpster fire: it's too long, he starts yelling, he makes demands, his jokes aren't funny, and he hangs up in disbelief over what he's just done. That's basically a description of the message I left for Chip.

"Hi, Chip, I'm Clint Harp," I began. "You don't know me, but I got your number from a friend . . . and I'm here to build furniture . . . and I'm going for my dream . . . you see, back when I was six . . ." And on and on I went. I probably rambled on about my grandfather, and how he'd inspired me, and how I'd quit my job to move to Waco and was hoping to have a carpentry shop someday.

Chip never called me back.

If we were financially stressed when we arrived in town, we were at the breaking point a few months later. At least during our leanest months before Waco, we'd been spending real money. Now we stayed afloat by maxing out our credit cards. What was I thinking, quitting a job with a great company and a potential nest egg north of a quarter million dollars if I'd been willing to diligently save? But no. Not me. I couldn't wait. I felt like the biggest idiot ever, like a failure as a husband and father. My confidence was gone. I'd jumped off a ledge with my arms stretched out wide and now I was frantically searching for the rip cord. But I hadn't even thought to strap on a parachute.

A day came when I realized how my foolish leap had ruined just about everything we'd worked so hard to attain. Kelly and I had reached for the stars and missed by a light-year. That afternoon, I drove over to a place I knew all too well: the dilapidated pink house.

Kelly had once wondered if maybe, just maybe, we could buy that house and bring it back to life. Shortly after first discovering it, we even called the Realtor, Camille, to discuss an offer. She was kind enough to sit down with us and hear both our story and our ridiculous offer, which was way below the asking price and came with zero guarantees that we could actually get someone to loan us the money. She was as kind as we were insane. We might've been broke, but at least we had vision to spare. For us, that pink house came to serve as a reminder of just how crazily hopeful we were. We'd had the audacity to think we could rub two sticks together, in the rain, in the cold, with no kindling and tired hands, and be lucky enough to spark a flame.

Maybe I went back to the pink house that day because I was trying to remember what it felt like to believe in a dream. It was from the overgrown lot of that house that I called my wife.

Like many others, I fight feelings of failure until I absolutely can't anymore. The funny thing is, it always seems that when I end the battle, the best things tend to happen. I think Kelly could hear the struggle in my voice that day, and after listening to me describe my stress through tears, she suggested that we forgo all plans for the day and just take the kids to the park.

A few minutes later, Kelly showed up with the kids, and off we went. We'd spent a lot of time at parks with our little family. This one was adjacent to the yard of a house where I'd lived during college, and in that yard, I'd kicked off my marriage proposal to Kelly years before. It was just the kind of connection we needed at that moment. We parked our car where I'd parked so many times before, lifted our kids out of the back seat, and found a bench. Kelly and I watched as Hudson and Holland, then five and two years old, built castles in the sandbox, whizzed down the slide, and soared high on the swings, oblivious to my meltdown. That day, it took all the energy we had to just sit there. But someone had once told us that if you didn't know the next step to take in a situation, you go back to what you know is right, and for us, that was always our family. We may not have known what to do financially, but we knew our kids could use some fresh air and playtime, and that was something we could give them. They played as Kelly and I looked on silently. I'm sure there was some discussion of what was or wasn't happening for us financially, but mostly, we were quiet. We had no answers.

An hour later, it was time to go home. When I got in the car, I noticed the gas light was glaring. I hate that light. We needed to fill up. There are a lot of gas stations in Waco. But on this day, for whatever reason, I chose to go to the one on Wooded Acres in the parking lot of the H-E-B grocery store. And I chose the pump right at the end of the line, with my car facing the road. I paid for the gas, stuck the nozzle in, and got back in the car to wait.

When the tank was around half full, a big black truck turned into the gas station and drove right in front of us. On the side of that truck was a logo that read "Magnolia Homes." I looked at Kelly.

"Isn't that the company of the guy I called and left that ridiculous message?"

"Yep, I think so," she said.

Hail Mary time.

The truck pulled in and parked on the other side of my pump. A man got out. I got out, too, and approached him. "I'm Clint," I began, "and I left a message for a guy named Chip a few months ago, about how I wanted to build furniture, and . . ."

He stuck out his hand. "I'm that guy," he said. "I'm Chip Gaines."

As soon as I made the connection, I went right back into dumpster-fire mode, reprising that awful voicemail. "No way!" I said. "Wow! That's crazy, 'cause I was just sitting there in my car wondering what in the world my next step is, 'cause you see, I quit my job a few months back and I was thinking that I could build some tables, but nothing is happening, and . . ."

Chip stopped me so he could ask some questions and fill in a few gaps, and probably also to shut me up. For years, he told me, he and his wife, Joanna, had also been building their own company, flipping houses and selling home goods. "I'll tell you what," he said after a couple of minutes of small talk, "why don't you drop your family off at home and then stop by my shop and maybe we can chat some more?"

We didn't know each other at all, but somehow, that afternoon, we ended up driving around Waco for three hours just talking. He showed me some projects he and his wife were working on. I told him about quitting my job. He told me about their new development. I explained I was volunteering with Habitat for Humanity. He said that they had four kids. At the time, we had two. He built houses. I wanted to build furniture. On top of being an interior designer, his wife had been selling the home goods she curated to anyone who'd buy them, and she was hoping to add a furniture line. Kelly was pursuing her master's but had previously designed baby clothes and home goods and had a great eye for home décor. They didn't quite know where their lives were headed. Neither did we.

Chip suggested that our family come over for dinner, and a few nights later, we did. We knocked on their door and sat down together for a spaghetti meal while our kids ate and played in the back. Around that table, the four of us just dreamed aloud together, and throughout the evening, Chip popped in with, "You know, I feel like there could be something more here." More sounded good, more of anything. More food? Yes, please. More conversation, more time, more planning? Absolutely.

That evening, Joanna asked me, "Clint, do you think if I drew up some designs on a piece of paper, you could possibly build them?"

I had no shop. I had no lumber. I had some tools, but they were in storage. I'd built a few tables and one bed, for which I'd earned zero dollars. I had a lathe, but didn't know how to use it—not yet, anyway. I really had little to offer.

"You bet, Jo," I told her. "I'm all in."

It would've been completely understandable for Kelly to shoot me a glance that meant "Say no, Clint! This girl clearly knows what she's doing and you definitely do not!" But Kelly didn't say a word. From across the table, she just looked at me like "Yeah, do it. I know you can."

I still can't believe I bumped into Chip, a guy who had no idea he was about to get his own TV show in less than a year from that day at the gas station. Some might call it providence, luck, serendipity, or even destiny. I'm not quite sure what to call it, but I do know this: what followed was as much a beginning as it was another step in the wild ride I'd been on for decades. And yet as extraordinary as this new chapter would ultimately be—eventually leading to our little startup, Harp Design Co., becoming known across the country through the hit HGTV show *Fixer Upper*—for me, the real story is all that came before. And that story starts with a bucktoothed kid from Atlanta who didn't think he was headed anyplace special. Sometimes life has to fall to pieces for the journey ahead to become incredibly clear.

CHAPTER 2

Splintered

By the time I begin a project, I've already dreamed about the finished product enough. It's now time to start making that dream a reality. One step is all that matters. Where that step leads is not for you to worry about. One step, one day, one board, one nail, one drop of sweat. When I drown out all the other noise and find this rhythm, things start to happen. If you can do this, you'll find yourself in your moment, ready to craft something that will last, in some form, forever.

Just off the banks of the Chattahoochee River, right outside of Atlanta, sits another house. It's the home that my grandfather Verner Martin built. We called it the Buzzard's Roost, or, for short, simply the Roost. During my early childhood, the Roost was my favorite place in the world. I did a lot of growing up there. It was a kid's paradise, complete with a pool, peacocks roaming the yard, and plenty of land for make-believe adventures. Off the kitchen sat a nine-foot yellow pine table my grandfather built with his crew when they constructed the home. We always ate around that table, looking out on the Chattahoochee through the bay window at one end.

It was at the Roost that the curtain goes up on my memory. I was three and a half. There I sat, at the top of my granddad's stairs, waiting for my mom to marry my stepdad in the living room below.

I was the ring bearer and wore a white suit and rust-orange tie, with my hair feathered to the right. My sister Bonnie, then six and the wedding's flower girl, sat next to me in a flowing white dress, her body covered in chicken pox. She held a doll, which she clutched tight. I played with a toy airplane, proudly showing it to my uncle David and aunt Suzanne, who had just started her decades-long run as a flight attendant for Delta Airlines. For the longest time, I had thought my aunt gave me that toy plane. But years down the road, I would learn that my airplane and Bonnie's doll had been a peace offering from our stepdad-to-be.

The night before the ceremony, we'd stayed at his apartment. Mom wasn't with us. She tells me now that he gave us those toys as a way to ease the coming transition. In the cool indie movie of my life that plays in my head, I like to imagine my sister and me saying, "All right, let's cut the crap, Jim. We barely know each other, and we're probably not ready to do this. But let's buckle down and figure it out, okay?" We'd then grudgingly accept his presents, eat a snack, and maybe stare, in awkward silence, around at his seventies-themed apartment. What really happened is that we took those gifts and loved them, with no idea of all that was to follow.

I can still see myself at the top of those stairs, holding that plane. I remember what the metal felt like in my hand. I remember wanting to fly. I remember that I held on to that little plane for the rest of that day and for years to come. I've since wondered what must've been going through the heads of my aunt and uncle as they waited there with us. Maybe they were reflecting on our family's history, with all its twists and turns. Or maybe they were thinking how much our mother and father loved us and wanted the best for us, even if their best didn't always turn out as expected.

* * *

My biological parents, Trish and Barry, split up when I was three and my sister Bonnie was six. I've never looked into the details really, probably because I didn't truly want to know. They couldn't make it work, and that was that. Soon after their divorce, both remarried, and Bonnie and I lived with our mom and new stepdad, Jim. A few months after the wedding, he got a job in Asheville, North Carolina, so the four of us left Atlanta and moved there.

Every other weekend and for the next eight years, Bonnie and I were loaded into the back seat of our car so my mom and stepdad could drive about two hours to the halfway point between Asheville and Atlanta—a Kentucky Fried Chicken in Clayton, Georgia. There, my stepdad would pull into one side of the lot and park. Mom would then hug and kiss us good-bye, hand us our bags, and send us off to walk about thirty yards across the lot to where my dad and stepmom, Linda, waited. It was your basic prisoner exchange. Bonnie was usually crying. She hated the send-offs.

For me, they were an early lesson in coping and emotional survival. Year after year and through trial and error, I figured out how to take the edge off a tense situation, how to smooth and rearrange the unhinged pieces of my life. *My dad likes it when I call my stepdad "Jim" instead of "Dad." My mom wants to feel like I always have a better time at home in Asheville than at my father's place in Atlanta. Get those things right, and you'll be okay.* Whether my assessments were right or wrong, that's how I managed the uncertainty, the stress, and the anxiety that followed my parents' breakup. I set up an emotional swap meet that involved saying exactly what I needed to say to keep things calm. I got really good at quickly sizing up others and taking their emotional temperature. *What makes that person explode? Noted. What makes him laugh? What makes her smile? Okay. Do that again.* I learned to make friends and make peace and make a rough road smooth, and by age six, I was pretty well versed in it. So good, in fact, that later in life, I'd be hired by a company in Houston to do that very thing.

Despite the twice-monthly weekend shuffle, I settled into life in Asheville. The town, nestled in the Blue Ridge Mountains, was magical in the fall, when the changing leaves blanketed the hills above it. I attended Haw Creek Elementary and played baseball at the East Asheville Ballpark. School, sports, hanging with friends, and Sunday church filled my days. I was the ultimate uncool kid: skinny, with protruding front teeth and an enormous head. Years later, a friend joked that I looked like a watermelon on a toothpick. I wore second-hand clothes, including a pair of tight red sweatpants that made my butt look even bigger than it already was. Though my family never missed a meal thanks to the relentless efforts of my stepdad, I knew we looked poor. Sounded poor. Dressed poor. Drove broken-down cars that often left us hoping for a miracle on the roadside. And we didn't own any of the homes we lived in like my friends did. Ever.

With things always so tight, Mom's parents would give us some extra cash whenever we visited Atlanta. But back home in Asheville, we were on our own. I'm sure my mother's parents figured she needed to make her own way in the world. Her father, the trailblazing builder that he was, had done it, and he required no less of his children. My own father, who worked in the finance department for Georgia Power, sent $250 a month in child support. Yeah, it wasn't much for two kids, but it's what he had and what he and my mom had agreed to.

Money or no money, poor or not, there's one reality that pretty much sums up my childhood: moving. The position my stepdad relocated for didn't work out, so from then on, he did any odd job he could, from selling carpets, to being the guy that essentially pushed the play button on a VCR to make sure a local UHF channel's shows kept playing, to working as a church facilities manager, in order to make ends meet. Really and truly, he worked his butt off. Mom's job, other than a handful of short-lived part-time gigs, was tending to Bonnie and me, and years later, to the two children she and Jim had: my sister Suzanne, who is seven years younger than me, and my brother, Ben, who is fifteen years my junior. And then even farther down the road in 2005, welcoming an adopted child to our family, Miracle. But regardless of how hard they worked, there was no stopping the seemingly never-ending game of musical houses.

During our eight years in Asheville, we moved eight times. We'd move around the corner or down the street or just about anywhere a landlord would take us. While there were plenty of other kids in my school whose families had as little money as we did, it seemed like most of them had what we lacked: stability. "You've lived in one house your whole life?" I once asked a classmate incredulously. As a child who relocated at least once a year and was shuttled across state lines twice a month, that blew me away.

But you know what? Moving was a freakin' blast. And you know why? Because my mom made it that way. She could figure out how to turn even the worst situation into an insanely good time filled with more laughter than you could stand. If there wasn't enough money to buy us new school clothes, she'd make a trip to the Goodwill feel like a carnival. If you moved houses with my mom, you'd have thought digging through dumpsters for packing boxes was the only way to do it. She was always laughing, always forging ahead.

Passionate, emotional, dramatic, kind, and caring—that's my mom. If some people wear their emotions on their sleeves, she coordinates a whole outfit. She'll give the shirt off her back to help a stranger and wants nothing more than to bond with anyone in her path. And, like I've said, the woman can laugh. I've never known a day where she hasn't, at some point, doubled over in hysterical laughter.

As the only daughter in her family, she worshiped her older brother, Howard, and adored her younger brothers, David and

Dean. Her mother, Ann Callaway Martin, a charming and smart Southern lady with the most beautiful eyes, was brilliant with a quiet inner strength. She was my mother's North Star. And yet what Mom craved most was the attention and affection of her father, which, to be fair, wasn't the easiest thing for a man who had gone through the things he had to give. He probably felt like he gave enough in the form of a beautiful house in a great area and food on the table at all times. But my mom craved more from the leading man in her life, and never really received it, so just out of high school, she eloped with a guy she hardly knew and began living a nightmare she initially kept to herself. Nine months into the marriage, she shocked her parents with a revelation: "Mom, Dad, he's beating me."

Now, my granddad was by no means a perfect father, but I dare you to mess with that man's family. Though he didn't always show it, he cared deeply. No one knew exactly how my grandfather intervened, but he did. Let's just say the marriage was quickly annulled, and no one heard from the guy again. Mom enrolled in college, completed a two-year degree, and tried to get her life back on track.

My grandmother, proud of her daughter's progress, nudged her forward.

"Honey," she said to her one evening, "I dare you to go to the singles event this weekend at church."

"I don't know," my mother said. "It's just not time yet."

"Trisha, do it," she insisted. "Just go."

Mom went. And that was the day Patricia Ann Martin met a man named Barry Kenneth Harp—my father.

My dad is something. He was the eldest of three, with his two sisters, my loving aunts Malinda and Donna Lee, trailing close behind. A disciple of Jackie Gleason and Johnny Carson, he can't help but crack a joke. His dad, my granddad Donald, was the same way. Like Granddad Donald, my father lit up every room he stood in, including that church hall where he first noticed my mother, with her beautiful eyes, flowing black hair, and olive-toned skin.

Dad was in the air force, and by the time he met my mother, he had finished stints in Thailand and Maine. Out of high school, he'd attended a couple of community colleges but hadn't been too sure what he wanted to do with his life. After he'd stumbled through a few courses, his draft number was called. Had he not been enrolled as a student, he would've been sent to Vietnam, right at the height of the conflict, as an army man—which would've forever changed his trajectory. But thankfully, he didn't have to go. Then, at twenty-one, he entered military service by his own choice. He signed up with the air force and spent time in basic training in San Antonio, Missouri, Oklahoma, and New Hampshire before being shipped off for about a year in Thailand. As a security officer, he protected the gate to the base until, in October 1969, President Nixon started calling troops home. My dad fortunately got to relocate to Maine—because two weeks after he'd gone, his base in Thailand was attacked.

With a broad smile, a square jaw, and an uncanny resemblance to Prince Charles, my dad to this day talks about his time in Maine and his stint in the service as if he just returned. He remembers it so vividly. He'd married a woman in Maine, but when things didn't work out between them, they divorced and he returned to his hometown of Atlanta. Two months following the divorce, my dad's friend invited him to a singles event at his church. And there was my mom.

After meeting at that church party, my parents' connection was instantaneous. The two became inseparable as their feelings for each other grew. My mother recounts my dad, who was not quite the romantic, doing his best to explain his love for her by saying, " 'I love my mom, my sisters, and you—in that order . . .' " Well, at least he was clear, and apparently it was enough to capture her heart. Soon after that, they married.

A mother's dare and a friend's invitation—that's why I'm sitting here. My mom tells me now that when she met my dad at the singles event that evening, she'd needed to laugh, and he had cracked her up. They both needed to feel loved and found it in each other. But six years into their marriage, the shared laughter was replaced with arguments, the humor and love with disdain. My mother called it quits. Though they're at peace now, the anger and hurt between them would last for years and create scars that would never go away. Yet out of all of it, two things were created that neither regretted. My sister Bonnie. And me.

*　*　*

During visits with my dad in Atlanta, I slept on the living room couch; Bonnie shared a room with our new stepsister, Becky, who was about seven years older than me. I was allowed to sleep on Becky's waterbed once. I wet it. Back to the couch.

My dad, an avid Georgia Bulldogs fan, loved sports. On the weekends when I was in town, we played baseball, football, and basketball till he was probably ready to collapse. And then there was tennis. Some of my best memories are of Dad taking me to the courts down the street from his house. There, he patiently taught me how to play, first just on the service court and then, when I was older and more skilled, on the full court. That one-on-one time meant the world to me. During the fall, we watched the Bulldogs on TV and went to a few games in Athens. Once we even dressed head to toe in UGA gear and posed for family photos. Neither of us would ever attend UGA, but to this day, we both bleed red and black.

Fridays were square dance nights. Someone always brought deviled eggs, and I always ate them (to this day, my stepmom, Linda, will make sure there are deviled eggs for me at any family get-together). Saturday mornings was church league bowling. Dad would rent our shoes and buy Bonnie and me a couple of games. One lane over from us, he would be making a spectacle of himself. He'd toss the ball with all his strength and then he'd try to will it toward the pins using bizarre facial expressions and hilarious sound effects as Bonnie and I burst into laughter.

If not dancing, bowling, or playing in the yard, we were usually visiting Dad's parents, Granddad Donald and Grandmom Camille. On the many nights when all the Harps gathered at their place, my grandmother made it her mission to keep us well fed, always asking, "Anybody want a roll?!" She'd cook up a Southern feast in the kitchen, while in the living room my cousins and I would crowd around my grandfather. "Pull my finger," he'd say, offering it to me with a grin. Once I did, he'd pull me in close and squeeze the life out of me till I couldn't take it anymore. I loved those hugs. I could hear his heartbeat and smell his aftershave. Then I'd get my turn at riding his leg like a horse. Those were good days.

Spending time with Dad and my extended family was fun, but I still hated the back and forth. As I got older and became more involved in school activities, it got tougher. I felt constantly split in two, as if I were always disappointing one or both of my parents. If, for instance, some cousins on my mom's side were coming to Atlanta and staying at my grandparents' house, I'd have to choose whether to skip my weekend with Dad and stay with Mom, which created in me a painful tug-of-war. Did my parents mean well? You bet. Did I feel caught in the middle, as so many children of divorce do? Absolutely.

On the plus side, because of all the time I spent in Atlanta during summer vacations and weekends at my grandparents' place while still living in Asheville, Georgia still felt like home. In some ways, I preferred it. The pace of life in Atlanta matched my stride. People were busy there. My cousins and friends spoke without the thick country accent I'd picked up in Asheville. Their parents took them to the mall and drove nicer cars. They lived in one place and didn't wear hand-me-downs. For me, Atlanta was a window onto a different way of life—and as time went on, it was a life I wanted.

My take was that Dad used humor to cope with the general disarray that comes with a family spread across two states. Every night, he stayed up late to watch *The Tonight Show Starring Johnny Carson*, and when I was in town he let me watch, too. We'd sit together as Johnny tucked the world into bed with punch lines, and Dad would tap out a beat on his knee with one drumstick while laughing hysterically at some ridiculous joke made by Carson or his sidekick, Ed McMahon. Years later, married and with kids of my own, I still watch *The Tonight Show*. Jimmy Fallon is now the host, but the feeling is still the same. And as I watch and laugh and forget about all the stress that comes along with life in general, I realize why I think my father loved the show so much, or at least one of the reasons. For an hour and a half, he could turn off every-thing—the pain, the stress, the sadness, and the disappointment of a home broken in two—and we could laugh.

Back in Asheville, my life and my weekends centered around church. Sure, we went to Sunday services with Dad in Atlanta at the historic, stained-glassed Peachtree Christian Church whenever we were in town, but when it came to my spiritual instruction, that was Mom's domain. She was raised a staunch Southern Baptist and brought us up in the same tradition. As I see it, every denomination, religion, and ideology comes with its own pluses and minuses, as well as its own interpretations of what is thought to be best. I happened to be raised in what you might call a very "Thou Shalt" and "Thou Shalt Not" tradition where the truth, as outlined in Scripture, was black and white, with little room for gray in those days. Praying before meals was required and quite possibly even ensured us against poisoning. I wasn't sure. Children disobeying their parents was akin to murder. Weekly church attendance was mandatory. Cursing, smoking, and drinking were what "unsaved" people did and most definitely off the table. And if a movie contained even the slightest off-color moment, Mom made us cover our eyes, which means I watched most movies through the cracks of my fingers. The world as I knew it back then revolved around two basic questions: "Are you a Christian?" and if so, "Are you good at it?"

At age eight, with no doubt a tablespoon of loving pressure from my mom, I officially "said the prayer" and "accepted Jesus into my heart." More than anything, my mother wanted to be sure her children were saved and going to heaven, and that proclamation was, for her and many others in the faith, the only marker of certainty. I have to admit that half of me did it for Jesus and the other half did it for my mom. "Clint's become a Christian," she announced to my stepdad as she prepared a budget-friendly snack of apples and peanut butter. That was our big celebration, and to this day, it's still one of my favorite treats, and maybe also why I get so hungry whenever I talk about God.

My mother raised us with love and Christianity, but her greatest dream and most heartfelt ambition were tied to her faith. As far back as I can recall, she wanted to be a Christian music star like Amy Grant or Sandi Patty. A love for music runs through both sides of my family: Mom was a singer, Dad a drummer, and my uncle David, Mom's brother, was an accomplished singer/songwriter. In the early nineties, he even moved to Canada and started a band, Hemingway Corner, with two other guys. It was a success for over a decade. Mom spent much of my childhood trying to land a record deal. At home, she'd pluck away at the strings of her acoustic guitar for hours, writing her own songs with the hope of a breakthrough. On weekends, we'd follow her to any and every church service or revival where she might be allowed to grab a mic.

When it came to finding that big break, Mom would do anything. Or almost anything. Late one Sunday evening, we drove into the backwoods of North Carolina to attend another revival, and I slept the whole way. By the time I awakened, Mom was climbing back in the van. As we drove away, I spotted a folding table in front of the church with boxes stacked on top of it.

"What happened, Mom?" I asked, rubbing my eyes.

"Honey," she said, a bit out of breath, "you know I don't do snakes!"

"Snakes?" I asked, shifting toward her to be sure I'd heard her correctly.

"Yes, babe, snakes," she confirmed as my stepdad gripped the wheel and barreled forward. "Those boxes on that table were full of them. We're gone!"

Serpents were just about the only thing that kept my mom from singing. It was all she'd ever wanted to do, and she definitely had great vocal talent. Though she never did achieve her ultimate dream, she never stopped trying. Even now, if you give that lady a mic, she'll sing. And if it's your birthday, get ready, 'cause you're getting a song on your voicemail.

*   *   *

When I was around the age of ten, my granddad Donald became very ill. Bonnie and I were rushed from Asheville to Atlanta to visit him in the hospital before he died. Diabetes had not only ravaged his body but also robbed him of his disposition. Gone was the riotous laughter. In its place was a frail man who barely spoke. Two days after we saw him, he was gone too soon, at age sixty-five.

Life was different after that day. An emptiness and sadness would hang over the Harp family for years to come. As much moving as

I'd done in my life, it was hard to move on from this loss. I couldn't imagine my life without Granddad Harp. Who was going to let me stay up late and watch wrestling and eat icing straight out of the container? Who was going to welcome me at the front door the way he did, with arms thrown wide and a big smile on his face? At first I was too stunned to cry, but once I saw my grandfather laid out in his casket, the dam broke. I leaned against my stepsister, Becky, and sobbed. And though I didn't know it at the time, my mother watched me quietly from the back of the church. Despite the bitterness that had flowed between her and my father, she'd loved Donald, too, and had secretly showed up to say good-bye.

The next year brought with it another big shift. The work my stepfather had been piecing together dried up, and when he could no longer make the rent, our landlord served us an eviction notice. Mom reached out to her parents that evening. Lying in bed with the door cracked, I overheard bits of the conversation.

"Hi, Mom and Dad. . . .Yeah, not good. . . .We just don't know what else to do. . . . Move in with you? Well . . . I mean . . . Yes."

While it was a pretty tough day for my mom and stepdad, as far as I was concerned, we couldn't pack the moving van fast enough. There's a scene in the movie *Rudy* where the head coach of Notre Dame's Fighting Irish football team finally asks Daniel "Rudy" Ruettiger to play in a game. Rudy runs onto the field with arms outstretched, and all of South Bend stadium goes wild. That night I felt exactly like Rudy in that stadium. We were moving to Atlanta. My way out of Smallville. Yes, I hated to leave my friends and my school, and Asheville's a beautiful place (and became an even greater town in the years that followed . . . to this day, I still visit there and love it), but I was already gathering up the scraps of my chaotic two-state existence and dreaming of a brand-new life. I knew that greater things lay ahead for me. I was right.

CHAPTER 3

Setting Up Shop

*My first shop was my backyard. My first tools were a miter saw,
a circular saw, a hammer, and a drill. Everything I've built to
this day started in that backyard, with those few tools. What I
lacked, I eventually acquired. What I didn't know, I learned.
What I messed up, I fixed. But what I never started, I never saw
come to life. I'm now surrounded by planers and jointers, lathes
and sanders, but it all comes down to where and how you start.
Throw it all on the table, take stock, set up shop—and begin.*

My mother's father, Verner Martin, was a self-made man and entrepreneur. Back in the late 1950s, after returning from his post as a
navy signalman in the Second World War, he started a shipping
supply company called Martin Packaging in Atlanta, Georgia. With
some inherited money of my grandmother's, he not only started
the business but he also had the foresight to invest in property: he
bought up acres of land around Dunwoody and Sandy Springs,
which would become some of the most sought-after areas on the
outskirts of Atlanta as the years went by. On one large plot of that
land, right on the edge of the riverbank, he built the Roost. From
the foundation up, he constructed the entire thing by hand, with
a small crew that even included my uncles.

Granddad Martin was a builder. Whether that meant launching
his own business, erecting the walls of the Roost, or constructing

a table, he knew how to create something from nothing. After he purchased all that land, he began constructing custom homes on it. He had no formal training, but he knew how to figure things out. Once, when he decided his style would be colonial, he visited Virginia and studied the houses there, taking detailed notes and pictures and measurements. He then returned home to replicate the design. That was his training.

In addition to his natural handyman skills, he also possessed a strong work ethic, a fierce independent streak, and an insatiable desire for exploration. If my granddad wasn't building a house, he was flying down to Mexico to mine for gold and do God knows what else. I got those genes, the ones that led him to build things, strike out on his own, and chase damn near impossible dreams. While most everybody else around him had jobs they reported to daily, my granddad could wake up, get on his bulldozer, and work his own land. I loved that. And even as a boy, I knew I wanted that kind of freedom. I also knew I wanted to one day work with my hands.

Verner taught me the value of hard work. He took me to his work sites and gave me jobs—small, often menial tasks, but they were my first real taste of responsibility. He bought me my first work boots and taught me how to swing a hammer, work heavy machinery, and properly mow the grass. Sometimes I'd drill holes through studs in the wall so he could run electrical and plumbing; other times, I'd hang insulation or drag 2x4s to wherever he needed them. I was basically his assistant whenever I was on the site. "Hey, cowboy," he'd say when I was mowing the lawn, using the nickname he always called me, "you have to pick up all the sticks in the yard first." I'd walk in parallel lines, end to end, to retrieve the branches before dragging the mower across the lawn. "Good job, cowboy," he'd tell me, patting me on the shoulder with his heavy hands after inspecting my work. It wasn't enough to do the job. It had to be done right.

I learned from my granddad by trailing him. There I'd be, wide-eyed and eagerly at his side, whenever he stepped onto a jobsite or into his tool shop. Anything he told me in passing, I took to heart. "If you're not careful when using an auger bit with a corded drill," he once said, "you'll break your wrist." To this day, I don't grab a corded drill without hearing him saying that. One afternoon when my stepdad was laying wood floors for my grandfather and I was giving a hand, Granddad came in and poured sand all over the floor. "Once everyone steps on the sand," he explained, "that'll naturally take away the softer wood, raise the grain a bit, and give the wood a beautiful look." He was always teaching me and always encouraging me to get the job done right.

The summer after we moved to the Roost from Asheville, my cousin Michael came down from his home in Ohio to live there, too. He was interning at the Carter Presidential Library, where my grandmother worked. At the time, I was eleven and Michael was ten years older. He was tall like his dad, my uncle Howard, and built pretty thick as well. He listened to edgy music, stayed up late, was incredibly intelligent, and watched movies I was never allowed to see. I was pretty stoked to be sharing my uncle Dean's old room with him. After so many changes in my life, it felt good to be hanging out with family in a house that didn't seem to be going anywhere.

One weekend, my grandfather noticed Michael and me just sitting around, and he decided to give us some work. "All right, here's what I want," he said. "Clean all the dog crap off the side porch over there. Make sure the yard is free and clear of all sticks so you can mow the lawn, Clint. And clean up the woodpile; basically just restack the whole thing, as it's practically falling down. Get all that totally done. See you this afternoon."

Michael and I plugged away at the chores my granddad had left us. It was hot and humid, as summers usually were, especially when you lived right on a riverbank. The porch was a mess, and cleaning it up sucked. Michael and I picked up most of the crap and then moved on to the sticks in the yard. This job was a little bit more ambiguous. It was a big yard. I was used to doing this particular job on my own, and my methodical system of walking up and down the yard, combing the entire thing and picking up every last stick, was very effective. But working with my cousin, I found myself following him aimlessly around, as I was more interested in sticking by his side than anything else. I had only one boy cousin other than Michael at the time, and he was a newborn; otherwise, I was surrounded by girl cousins (whom I love dearly!) on both sides. Hanging out with a guy, especially one as cool as Michael, was something I didn't want to miss out on.

After strolling around half the lawn and picking up maybe half the sticks, we were exhausted. And yet, as much fun as I was having being with Michael, I was starting to get a little worried about our job performance. By the time we got to the pile of logs stacked on the side of the carport, Michael said, "Screw it, I'm done," and went inside. To be fair, Michael already had a job, and quite frankly wasn't looking to work on the weekends, and I really couldn't blame him. But our grandfather couldn't have cared less. As for me, I was dying for my grandfather to entrust me with more and more responsibility. So with the thought of my granddad's disapproval in my mind, I stuck it out for a bit longer. Working my way around the logs, I stacked what I could on the already shaky pile and tried to make it look pretty. But then I heard music coming from inside the house. I thought, *Wait, if he's in there chilling out listening to music, why am I out here doing this?* And just like that, I walked off the jobsite. Hanging out with Michael was just too much to pass up.

Michael had the music blaring. He was into heavy metal at the time, and the volume was cranked up like I hadn't heard before. He was holding a beer.

"Hey, bud! Go grab yourself a Coke, man. That was a lot of work, you know? Yeah, grab a Coke. Shut it down."

Just as I cracked open the Coke can, I heard a faint sound like the opening and closing of a door.

Verner was home. And he hadn't just come home. My granddad had been there for a few minutes. When he pulled up, he'd decided to take a stroll around the yard to check out the job we'd done. By the time he walked inside, he was fuming. He laid into us like never before. It was humiliating. I had let the man down. And I knew it. Even before he got home, I knew I was wrong.

Years later, as I sat with my cousin Michael, now a successful lawyer with his own practice, at his dad's funeral, we dug back into the archive of memories. "You know," Michael told me, "I'm old enough to remember when your mom and dad were married. Before you were born."

"That's crazy!" I said. "You're right, I've never thought about that."

"Yeah, I remember your dad. I liked him. He was funny. Did you know he used to work with Granddad?"

My head could have exploded. My dad was a lot of things, but handy just wasn't one of them, so the thought of him working with my grandfather—well, I couldn't imagine it. Verner wasn't one for funny business, while my dad walks into a room with the sole purpose of making people laugh.

"Yeah, your dad used to help our grandfather out," Michael continued. "So there was this one time when your dad and my dad were working for Granddad. He told them to do a few things and at the end of the day make sure they parked the truck in a certain spot and closed the fence. Your dad backed up the truck, and as he did, he hit the fence and knocked it out of whack. My dad had kinda had it with Granddad for other various reasons, so he told your dad to park the car on the street and worry about it later. The next day when Granddad found out, he laid into our fathers like you wouldn't believe, kind of like he laid into us that summer. I don't believe your dad ever worked for him after that. And that's when my family decided to move away from Atlanta."

Michael's story made me see my dad, my uncle, and my cousin in a whole new light—and myself as well. That day, I learned a little bit more about who I was, the parts of me that are like my dad and the parts that are like my granddad. I realized that it was up to me to choose which part of myself to express. Ever since, when I have a job to do, I can hear my grandfather's voice saying, "Clint, do it right the first time, so you don't have to go back and do it again."

We ended up finishing the job our granddad asked us to do. It was no doubt humiliating having to go back and do it again, the very thing he taught me not to do. But I guess there's a lesson in there as well. If you do have to go back and do it again . . . do it. And do it well.

Mercifully my granddad ended up paying us for our work. And it's a good thing he did. With my cash in hand I bought a ticket with my uncle Dean to my first concert. We saw R.E.M. in downtown Atlanta at the Omni Arena. The opening act was the Indigo Girls, who sang a song called "Kid Fears" with R.E.M.'s lead singer, Michael Stipe, pitching in on vocals toward the end. "What would you give for your kid fears? . . . Replace the anger with the tide." The words would stick with me to this day and remind me to not let the anger, the pain, and the disappointment of my younger years be the thing to guide me into the future.

*   *   *

As it turned out, when our family relocated to the Roost in 1988, we stayed only a year. Most mornings, I would come down and find my grandfather sitting at that pine table, just staring out at the foggy river and thinking. I was too young to recognize all the layers of his life, but I could tell he was a haunted soul. He had a reputation as a scoundrel of sorts, and one who was no stranger to the bottle. Over the years, many arguments and complicated feelings swirled between him and his children. In 2015, after fifty years of not seeing a doctor, poor circulation and old age claimed his life. It was only then that hidden chapters of our family's history were uncovered. Hurtful chapters. And yet for me, despite it all, Granddad Martin was a pillar. With all the tension and uncertainty I'd experienced in my young life, he made me feel stable.

The year I was twelve, my grandfather lost his company when an employee he'd also trusted as a friend embezzled nearly all his and my grandmother's fortune. I'll probably never know exactly what happened with the business, but we were devastated to learn that he and my grandmother would also lose the home he'd built. The Roost was gone. Thankfully, he held on to the 240 acres of land he'd once purchased in Dahlonega, a small town in North Georgia and the state's first site of gold, which kicked off the gold rush in the late 1820s. He eventually built another home there for himself and Ann.

During our very last visit at the Roost, we came downstairs one day to find my grandfather sitting at the yellow pine table with a knife before him. "Carve out your names," he told us, his finger stabbing the table. "And when you're done here, go do the same thing in the attic." Each family member carefully scraped his or her initials in the location where we usually sat. When it was my turn, I dug right in. I wanted my mark to last.

That table is still in my family, sitting in a barn on what's left of my granddad's North Georgia property, and it's beautiful. It has scars all over it. Scrapes, cup rings, places darkened from the oil of our skin, notches, and our initials carved right into the pine along with everything else. That table tells our stories. You couldn't construct that kind of table in a week; it takes years for wood to weather like that. It was a table meant to bear the weight of a Thanksgiving feast, stand up under the stress of a family argument, live through spills, burns, stains, and messes. It sat there ready for friends, family, and strangers to pull up around it and lay everything out. And it bears the unskilled carving of a boy wanting to make his mark.

*   *   *

I was in the middle of the fifth grade when we first moved back to Atlanta. My sister Bonnie—a great student who'd always worked her tail off in school, even amid the upheaval of our early years—was in junior high. Because Dunwoody was a wealthy area, I went to a public school where even the hallways and bathrooms were shiny and new. The kids wore fashionable clothes and just flat out looked cool, which meant that with my buckteeth and generic T-shirts and sneakers, I was as out of place as I'd ever been (albeit before my time, no doubt!). It's one thing to be the new kid with the cool British accent. It's an entirely different matter to show up as the hillbilly whose front teeth enter the room a full ten seconds before he does. But what I lacked in presentation, I tried to make up for in humor and personality. Like my father and his dad, two born performers, I always had a good joke in my back pocket.

Though my appearance made me the perfect target for some brutal teasing, one kid liked me well enough. His name was John. "Hey, Clint," he said one afternoon during lunch, "I play baseball at this church. It's called Dunwoody Baptist. You should come check it out. Tryouts are soon."

"Seriously?" I said, searching for a hint of sarcasm in his face. There was none. "That would be great!" I said. "I'm in! I'll tell my mom today."

Just about every parent I know wants the same thing for his or her child: happiness. So the day I raced home to tell my mother that I might have the chance to play baseball in the Dunwoody Baptist rec league, she saw the excitement on my face, and she made it happen. At the time, my family was still looking for a church, and by the end of the season, we were members at Dunwoody Baptist. Our move back to Atlanta seemed to be working out.

Over the next several years, some things stayed the same, but a lot of things got better. Bonnie and I still spent every other weekend with our dad, but at least now it was a simple drive across town with a driveway drop-off in place of the prisoner exchange. We still moved from place to place, but it seemed we were moving up at least, thanks to my stepdad landing steady work as a car salesman. After we left the Roost and had lived in apartments for a couple of years, we moved into a two-story house within walking distance of Peachtree Junior High, the school all my friends from church attended. We rented, just like always, but the house felt more like home than any place had before. We stayed there for three years, a record length of time for us.

During junior high, I became very involved in the youth ministry at Dunwoody Baptist, often traveling to Panama City Beach in Florida for church youth camps, a trip gracious church members funded whenever my parents couldn't. It was at Dunwoody, from junior high through the end of high school, that the faith my mom had passed on to me started to become my own. I *believed*, even if just a bit too much. I was as staunch and earnest in those beliefs as I'd been taught to be, but to a fault with my own brand of stubbornness added for good measure. Take the one spring break when I heard some friends from my youth group drank some Smirnoff and Miller Lite. I nearly lost my mind. I'm most definitely not making a case for underage drinking, but let's be honest, it must have been a real blast for my friends seeing my judgmental, Bible-thumping eyes staring back at them when they returned from vacation.

The second I turned fifteen, I got a job as a bagger at a Kroger grocery store. The following year, I worked at my church's rec center, setting up the gym and fields for youth baseball, soccer, and basketball leagues. I used my earnings to buy nicer clothes and shoes and the occasional fast-food meal with friends. By this time I had braces, which my parents and grandparents had chipped in to pay for (though I'm pretty sure there was a final payment or two that was ignored . . . times were tough). My parents let me borrow their car as long as I bought my own gas. We were still living pretty close to the edge. And although some weeks I ended up handing over my entire paycheck to my parents so we could pay the bills, I was at least able to ditch the tight red sweatpants. Now, with a tiny trickle of personal cash flow, I was no longer a complete dork. I actually started to feel like a normal kid.

Midway through my sophomore year, we moved again (this time, out of our two-story house, which really felt like home), but thankfully not far enough away so that I'd have to transfer. By that point I'd finally made it to Dunwoody High School, and I had no intention of leaving! The place had it all: jocks, dorks, cheerleaders, varsity teams for every sport, pep rallies, homecoming parades, and prom. Most important, it had the greatest principal I've ever known in Jennie Springer. From her place of leadership, Mrs. Springer guided students and an incredible group of teachers from all different races, backgrounds, and cultures—certainly something that was otherwise rare for the suburbs of Atlanta—with an unmatched skill for creating wonderful harmony. I remember years later finding it quite hilarious and awesome that I, a kid from the "Deep South" of Georgia, was usually the one coming from a more diverse and progressive culture than the other kids I was meeting. Those high school days were some of the best of my life, and I wouldn't trade them for anything.

When it came to sports, I made the JV baseball team early on but didn't get to play much. But on the football team, I was a legend—not as a player, my mom wouldn't let me near a field given that I was born with a couple of minor heart issues, but as their number one fan. Win or lose, rain or shine, I was there to cheer on the team. After one rainy game, one of the players came up to me and said, "Hey, thanks for being out there tonight. In the locker room, Coach reminded us not to give up, just like you never give up on us." It was better than any touchdown.

Despite the love of sports I shared with my dad, athletics never took off for me. But just before my junior year, I woke up to a new love: music. That summer, I'd gone to my annual church youth camp. My friend Chris Rice, who was about ten years older than me, led our group in worship songs as he played the keyboard and guitar. I remember watching him and thinking, *If I could learn a few songs, I could maybe do what he's doing.* He spent his summers traveling and singing. What a life! I raced home and told Mom about my new dream. She immediately went to her room and came out with her beloved acoustic guitar. She then taught me the four chords almost every guitarist starts with: G, C, D, and E minor.

Later that summer, as we drove to Daytona Beach, Florida, for a budget-friendly family vacay (Mom wanted to get to the beach so badly, I swear she would've had us sleep in the sand, if need be!), I strummed my guitar in the back of our van the whole way. I'd learned as many songs as I could, a grand total of three.

When we returned home, I'd lie in bed at night, practicing in the dark so I'd learn to make eye contact with people as I sang, just like Chris did, rather than staring at the fret board and searching for correct finger placement. A few weeks later I asked our youth minister if I could sing in front of the group as worship leader, and he agreed.

Soon after that, I assembled a small band and we played every Sunday and Wednesday at church. From then through the end of high school, I was seldom without my guitar. I dreamed of writing songs like Chris did, moving to Nashville, and one day signing a record deal. If that didn't work out, I figured I could be a music minister. When it came to actual talent, I probably wouldn't have made it past the first round of *American Idol* auditions, but that didn't stop me. I am my mother's son.

* * *

Until I was at Dunwoody High, surrounded by kids who never doubted they'd go to college, I hadn't really thought much of what I was going to do after senior year. I had vague thoughts of either finding my way into ministry or maybe going to work for my granddad Martin. But discovering a passion for music and the positive influence of my high school pushed me to genuinely consider college. However, I was a C student at best—constant moving doesn't exactly lend itself to good homework habits—so I had zero hope for an academic scholarship. I knew neither of my parents could pay my way, and in fact, the option was never even discussed. It was assumed that if I went to college, I'd figure out how to get there on my own. I'd once spotted my stepdad's tax return, and that year, he'd earned around $20,000. Things were a bit better at my dad's house, with both him and my stepmom working, but not so much that they could cover the expense of a college degree. It was financial aid or bust.

In the spring of my junior year, my friend Eugene, the most lovable guy, with an unforgettable grin, met me for lunch at Applebee's by Perimeter Mall. He was a few years older and was already working toward his undergrad degree at Georgia Tech just down the road in downtown Atlanta.

"I heard you're thinking about Baylor," he said.

"Sort of," I said, fidgeting as I pretended to study the menu. I was, in fact, definitely considering Baylor, a large private university in Waco, Texas—a college that had become a kind of nexus point for Christians, particularly those from the South. But because of Baylor's expensive price tag, I was too embarrassed to admit to Eugene that the school was even on my list. He'd visited me in the apartment where my family had moved by then; the complex was surrounded by halfway houses. In other words, he knew our financial situation. Maybe I had it all wrong and he was going to suggest community college, but instead, he uttered a sentence that changed everything for me.

"Clint," he said, "my dad and I would like to fly you out to Waco so you can visit Baylor and check it out." I was stunned and grateful, and completely unaware of just how much his gesture would change my life forever.

My friend Chris, the worship leader from my youth group days whose singing career had inspired my dreams, happened to be in Texas when I visited Baylor that fall. He met me at the airport in Dallas and drove me down to Waco. It was an oven; even in October, Texas temperatures can soar into the triple digits. "Before we head to campus, I want to introduce you to Kyle, a friend of mine," Chris said as we drove down I-35. Kyle, he explained, was pursuing ministry just like I thought I would and could be a great connection for me as I navigated the years and classes ahead.

We pulled into Waco and stopped at a soccer field where Kyle was playing in a game with the club team. He made an instantaneous impression on me. Laid-back and welcoming, he looked like he'd just stepped out of a Gap ad, while I, stuffy and uptight, looked like I'd just come from church. Later, while hanging out at his house, I learned more about his experience as a student and what my life could possibly look like if I moved to Waco. By the end of our time, I thought, *If enrolling at Baylor means becoming like this guy, I'm in.*

That instinct was reinforced a short time later. You know that feeling you have when something just seems right? That's how it was when I stepped onto the Baylor campus later that day. The grass was so green. The trees lining the lawns were proud and strong. As I stood on the school commons, gazing up at Pat Neff Hall with its brick facade and golden dome, something whispered that I was home.

With no idea how I'd pay for college, I aimed high and applied for a scholarship from the school of music. But not only did I not land the scholarship, I wasn't even accepted into the music school. My stepdad suggested I study business instead. That sounded like death to me. I wanted to sing and play my guitar, make an album, meet people, climb an invisible ladder, and find my own way. But first I had to get to Waco no matter what, so I took his advice. The following spring, I received a thick envelope containing my letter of acceptance into Baylor. My only way there would have to involve the F word: *financial aid.* I easily qualified.

I graduated from Dunwoody High in May 1996. By then, the foundation for my future had been laid. I was ready to set up shop for the next stage of my life in Waco. I'd learned some tough lessons from the chaos and drama that ensues when any family splits, and I'd made good use of the tools I'd been given. And that fall, with my Bible in my suitcase and my guitar under my arm, I showed up on Baylor's doorstep carrying them all.

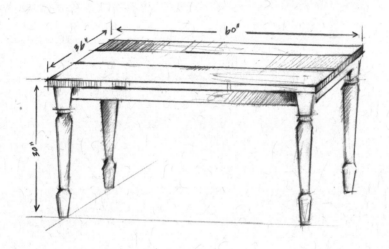

CHAPTER 4

Blueprints

I love journals. Especially cool leather ones that look like they could be a hundred years old. I must have a couple dozen of them sitting around my house. Some I've never written in, and some contain a few pages that hold my thoughts, ideas, and drawings. Once I feel inspired to build something, I pick up a journal and start a sketch. I scrawl out the dimensions, never drawing anything to scale but rather just mapping out how long and wide the table will be and how thick I'll make the legs. I usually draw a couple of angles of the table, with one featuring the side view and one from above. It's taken a while for me to get okay with the fact that my finished product will undoubtedly be different from my sketch, but taking the time to sketch out a dream isn't a waste of time. It's a plan—a blueprint for the way forward.

Emily and Laura, a couple of friends of mine who'd been like sisters to me back in our days growing up together in Dunwoody, were still just as dear to me as friends once we were all at Baylor. Early in my senior year of college I was invited over to see the new apartment they were sharing with some Baylor classmates. As Emily gave me a tour of their new digs, one of her roommates, a girl with green eyes, came walking down the stairs. "Oh, hey, this is Kelly," Emily said. "Kelly, this is Clint, our friend from back home in Atlanta."

I wanted to say something smooth, but all I could do was stare. For what felt like an entire minute, I stood there like an idiot thinking, *Wow, she's beautiful. Where has she been the last few years?* I'd later learn that while I was gawking, wondering how I'd missed this girl around campus, she was thinking this: *Hey, Clint. Yeah, I'm Kelly. We've met like four times before. No offense, but I really don't have time for this.*

"Hi, I'm, uh . . . Clint," I finally stammered, even though Emily had already said my name. So smooth.

"Nice to meet you," Kelly said. I stared some more as we exchanged small talk. I told her I was a senior, majoring in business and hoping to do something in ministry when I graduated. She was a junior, studying education, and she shared that she'd grown up in East Texas. I felt so drawn to her. From the moment I met Kelly—or at least from the moment I actually *recalled* meeting her—I knew I wanted to be around her.

In the weeks that followed, I made that happen. I spent more and more time at the apartment, under the guise of hanging out with Emily and Laura, and things began to heat up.

Now, for the record, Kelly actually asked me out first. Sort of. Her sorority, Chi Omega, was hosting a "date dash," an event for which members are told to invite two guys to a party at a club. You dance, get a free T-shirt, and just generally have good clean fun. On the one hand, it wasn't an "official date," but on the other, it turned out I was the only guy she invited. My confidence was on the rise. About a week later after that "first date," I found the courage to ask her to dinner. We talked until close to sunrise, the first of many late-nighters for us.

When you're falling for a girl, you want to know every detail about her—and I couldn't get enough of Kelly's story. The eldest of two girls in her family, she was born in Nacogdoches, Texas, before moving to Tyler, the Rose Capital of the World. Tyler is possibly the closest thing to a Southern city, the kind I was used to, that you might find in the Lone Star State. Beautiful azaleas grace the brick-paved streets of this town, which was built mostly from what most people refer to as "old oil money." Kelly had been quiet and shy but smart as a whip. If a fellow student was stumped by a question in class, she'd be the kid who knew the answer but wouldn't let on that she did.

Kelly loved art, and though she never studied it formally, she enjoyed creating beautiful things. Not long after we met, she showed me this massive art portfolio—filled with gorgeous paintings, sketches, and art pieces assembled using fabric and tissue paper— that she'd put together throughout high school. It was in summers, when Kelly's family drove down to Kerrville, a beautiful town in the Hill Country where they vacationed, that they took I-35 through Waco. From the back seat of their Suburban, she could see the gold dome rising over Baylor University and she would always think, *One day I'm going to that school.* Like me, she'd grown up Baptist, so the idea of attending a school with Christian roots appealed to her. And coincidentally, we had a friend in common: Kyle, the cool college senior I'd been introduced to on my first visit to Baylor. Kyle was also from Tyler, and after Baylor, he'd gone on to pastor at a Waco church called University Baptist, which Kelly ended up attending.

Back when Kelly was in high school, her mom was diagnosed with breast cancer. In the spring of 1993, after months of chemo, she finally kicked cancer's ass, but there was carnage from the battle. For years, Kelly's parents had struggled to keep their relationship right side up, and the cancer had made that tougher. Just before Kelly's fifteenth birthday, her parents split. Kelly, then a high school sophomore, had felt punched in the gut. Neighbors in a small town know pretty much everything about one another, and for a girl as private as Kelly, just being aware that people around town were talking about her family was incredibly painful. Eventually, Kelly's dad moved on and remarried, while Kelly and her sister stayed with their mom. It would take years for healing to even begin for their little split family of four, and even more for it to fully occur. But occur it did. And as I watched from a front-row seat as they hashed through pain and disappointment, I found myself amazed at what love, forgiveness, and humility can do.

The Thanksgiving after we met, as Kelly was preparing to travel to London to visit a friend who was studying there and I was gearing up to drive to Georgia, I said, "Why don't I drive up and stay at your mom's place to cut my trip in two?" Admittedly, I knew it would be smart to make a good impression on her family, and her mother, whom I had met previously in Waco, had been the first to suggest it anyway. Kelly agreed even though she'd already be across the pond by the time I got there. So on my cross-country drive from Waco to Georgia, I stopped in Tyler and met her mother, Debbie, and her sister, Johnna. We hit it off right away. I saw at once where Kelly's graciousness comes from: that lady fed me from sunup to dusk. Yes, food speaks to me. She also put me up in Kelly's bedroom. I remember looking around at her photos, thinking, *Who are these other guys in here?* I knew one thing: if there were any dudes in the background, I intended to be the last man standing. At least her mom and sister already seemed to be signing off on me.

The distance and time over Thanksgiving break definitely did the trick—we couldn't wait to reconnect. When we both got back to Waco, we officially became a couple.

It's funny how we're so often drawn to what we wish we had more of. Kelly tells me she was most attracted to my goofiness, spontaneity, and love of adventure and music. She always says I bring the fun. I was drawn to her smarts, sincerity, discipline, and desire for a true and honest connection. She was more organized than I will ever be. She was also definitely on the shy side, more introverted than I am by a mile. But even before I got to know her, I could tell there was a lot of depth and wisdom beneath the surface.

When it came to her religious beliefs, Kelly was also more moderate than me. In one of our early conversations, Kelly floated the idea that "becoming a Christian" didn't necessarily happen with one magical prayer, said at the end of an incredibly awkward and sometimes lonely walk down a long aisle to the front of a sanctuary filled with people who had already said the prayer. "Maybe becoming a Christian," she said to me, "is more of a journey. Maybe it's a lifelong quest of figuring out God, love, your purpose, God's purpose, in long and winding strolls through the many places life will take you."

Not a chance, I thought. That one prayer of salvation was everything. You have to have the prayer. Without it, pack your bags. Hell awaits. So Kelly and I had a nice argument over that one. And by argument, I don't mean two people debating their positions until they're blue in the face. In our case, arguing looked more like a dumb guy who thought he knew it all, doing his best to convince a very smart girl she was dead wrong. But the smart girl wasn't really into arguing. She was more of a sit-there-confidently kind of arguer, just patiently listening and then shooting an arrow in the form of a question that causes you to . . . wait for it . . . *think!* I clearly liked this girl, because despite what to me seemed like heresy, we kept on dating. And, well, she didn't run away either. But almost just as important as our relationship, consider the door of my own one-sided, narrow, and even dogmatic ways of looking at faith officially cracked open.

Sometime later Kelly told me she'd even sort of had her eye on me even before she arrived on Baylor's campus. I know . . . what??? Back home as a high school senior, she and a few other girls were hanging out at a friend's house, and that friend's sister was already at Baylor. They all noticed a picture on the fridge.

"Hey, who are these guys?" someone asked.

"One of them is Mark, my sister's new boyfriend," said her friend.

"And who's the other guy?"

"That's Mark's friend Clint. He volunteers with the youth ministry Mark runs."

"Well, that Clint guy's kinda cute," Kelly had said, smiling. "Let's make sure we meet him when we get to Baylor." And boy, did she.

Kelly and I dated for ten months before I proposed. It certainly wasn't unusual for a couple to get engaged before graduation, but I wanted my proposal to be remembered. So let's just say it began with me hiding in the bushes outside her house while my friend Scott read a poem I had written as a sort of invitation to a surprising day of adventure. I then took her to the zoo, of all places, and then it continued with her digging up, out of the ground, an outfit I'd bought for her to wear that evening. The proposal culminated with us driving down to Salado, Texas, just outside of Waco, where I'd had a friend bury the ring. I dug it up and presented it to Kelly as I popped the question. She said yes (well, technically she said okay . . . eh . . . close enough), even with my goofball proposal. And by the way, I'd committed to the digging theme as a way of saying, "Yeah, this whole relationship thing is going to be work, but if we dig together, we're going to make it." I probably could've just said all that and left the shovels out, but whatever.

Right after Kelly said yes, we both called our moms. I'd of course already asked Kelly's parents for permission to marry their daughter, and they'd approved. But while they and my own parents knew I was planning to propose, they didn't know when. So when Kelly and I dialed up our folks and excitedly told them we were engaged, it was a welcome surprise. We made a plan to tie the knot once we'd both graduated.

It's amazing how, during a lifetime, thousands of ordinary moments come and go without much notice. But then out of nowhere, an experience, a person, a turn in the road just grabs you by the collar. From then on, time is divided by all that came before that moment, and all that follows. Kelly, for me, is that marker.

*   *   *

My time at Baylor brought many good things, but academic success wasn't one of them. Yet there was one activity I excelled at during my tenure there: running. Back when I was around eight and visiting my family at the Roost, I'd beg my uncles to let me go out jogging with them. "Sorry, bud," they'd say, "you're too young, it's too hot outside, and we're going too far." I could still see them disappearing down the road without me, when, during my freshman year at Baylor, I began lacing up and running up to five miles at a time. I loved it, but never took it too seriously. Until the evening when a couple of my buddies, Mark and Ritchey, threw out an idea.

"Let's train for a marathon!" said Mark. We'd just stretched, and after a few swigs of water, taken off into the night for a run around Waco.

"Wait, what?" I said. "Are you serious? Isn't that like, twenty-six miles?"

"Absolutely," he said. "Let's do it." Ritchey, my best friend and roommate, was more reluctant. But, as it would turn out, his support would get me across the finish line as he ran miles with me, both in training and in the race.

That night, we ran farther than I ever had before, or even thought I could—eight miles—and I was hooked. For the next several months, I trained. I ran laps around campus and around town. I went from eating ice cream and pizza to a steady diet of chicken and potatoes. I used the money I earned delivering pizza to buy some running shoes and shorts. And as I ran, all my concerns seemed to melt away. My head cleared and worries dissolved. I wasn't breaking any records, but I was breathing my way through each step, racking up mile after mile. Childhood doubts, adolescent fears, and adult concerns all became less painful as, during what would become a theme of my life, I pushed myself beyond what I thought was possible. The following February, when I rounded the corner into the marathon's final mile and crossed the finish line, I collapsed on the street, feet swollen, out of breath, tired beyond reason—and absolutely sure I was going to run that race again.

As a junior, I did. By then, and on into my senior year, I had also started to think more seriously about my future. Academically, I'd barely scraped through Baylor with a GPA just north of a D and nearly $50,000 in student loans. Ouch. I still wanted to pursue music, but I figured that a full-time job with the youth ministry I'd been volunteering for, which had an opening in St. Petersburg, Florida, would make a great starting gig. It was an opportunity that would allow me to begin paying down my debt, and I was interested in seeing if the ministry was the path I was meant for.

All I had to do was complete my degree, which I was on track to do in the next few months. My final semester would be in the fall of 2000, the start of Kelly's senior year. Our plan was for me to earn my degree in December 2000 and take the job in Florida while she finished up in May. Then in July, we'd get married.

Of course, this timeline hinged on me passing all my remaining classes. I was a little worried about one senior-level business management class, but otherwise, I was packing my bags. My professor, though stern, seemed like a nice and fair man. "There are only a few requirements for passing my class," he told us on day one. "Pass all three tests and complete one assignment, which is due at the end of the semester." Easy enough.

Test one rolled around. I hadn't studied. I'd like to offer the disclaimer that when I was a kid, the basic understanding between my mom and me was pretty simple. I'd crawl home with another D+, and she'd say, "Honey, don't worry about it! You know I had to repeat the fifth grade because I couldn't understand math. Do your best." She meant well. What can I say . . . we were all just surviving back then.

Anyway, I took the first test, praying for a miracle. My professor had a funny way of revealing our grades. He'd use an overhead projector and cast our scores up on the wall. He wouldn't use names, just the scores. The first score was at the top; that one was important since he graded on a curve. All the other scores would be listed in descending order beneath the first. I sat in the front row, which was about the only thing I did right in that class. Standing near to me, the teacher turned on his projector to reveal this:

98

96

92

90

84

83

82

81

81

75

68

.

. .

.

24

Crap.

I immediately knew which score was mine. After class, I marched straight to the professor's office. "Excuse me, sir," I said in my most respectful tone. "Can we please talk?"

"Sure, come on in," he said, motioning for me to take a seat.

"Well, I've done the math," I began slowly, "and with only two remaining tests, there's literally no way for me to pass your class."

"Let me see here," he said, shuffling through a stack of papers on his desk and fishing out one. "Oh, yes. You must be Clint Harp. I'm guessing that wasn't your best effort."

"No, sir," I said. "It wasn't."

"Well, son," he said. "I don't know what to tell you."

This wasn't the first time I'd had a conversation like this. The year before, my finance professor had told me that my chances of passing were about as good as those of a—and I quote—"one-legged man in an ass-kicking competition." Message received. In that case, I'd eked out a D. But this class was different. My grade on that first test could have literally been the difference between a diploma in my hand and an extended career as a Baylor student. I'm sure Kelly would've found that attractive. Besides, I'd already nailed down the Florida gig. I had a job waiting. I was also an eternal optimist, incredibly confident that I could talk my way out of just about anything, so I tackled the situation head on.

"I'm so sorry," I told him. "I'm just embarrassed, and I feel awful."

"I'm sure you do," he said, laying the paper on his desk and staring at me.

"The thing is," I continued, "I already have this job in Florida, and it starts right after I gradu— Well, *if* I graduate. You know what I'm saying."

"Sounds like one heck of a predicament," he said, no trace of give in his voice.

"Yes, sir, it is," I said. "If I don't pass your class, I'm in trouble.

Please. I'll do anything." I was creeping into the early stages of hyperventilation.

The professor took off his reading glasses, folded them on his desk, leaned back in his chair, and thought for a moment.

"I'll tell you what," he said finally. "You've got two more tests and a homework assignment. Pass both tests and get a better score on the third than the second, plus do the one homework assignment, and I'll pass you."

"Oh my goodness, sir, thank you!" I said, rising to shake his hand. "Thank you so much! I won't let you down."

The second test rolled around. I studied a bit and was pumped when I managed to earn a passing score of 60. How sad. For the next and final test, I put in a decent amount of study time. *I'm going to really impress him*, I kept telling myself. In class, I held my breath as he flashed the final scores up on the wall. I'd earned a 61. I'd passed—or so I thought.

Walking home that day, I felt I could finally exhale. *A 61? Not the greatest show on earth, but it's enough to get me to the next step on my journey with Kelly.* I got to my apartment and was excited to call Kelly and let her know the good news, but that's when I spotted a note my roommate had left for me by the phone.

"Hey, Clint," it read, "call your guidance counselor."

She must want to congratulate me on finishing, I thought. I dialed the number.

"Hi, this is Clint!" I said enthusiastically. "You called?"

"Yes, Clint," she said. "So, your business management class. Did you know you failed it?"

Big gulp.

"Um, I mean, no," I stuttered. "I didn't."

By this time, two things were definite. First, with the graduation ceremony just days away, my parents were already on the highway heading to Waco. And second, my job was starting in exactly three weeks. With my blood pressure through the ceiling, I hightailed it to my professor's office.

"I just got a call from my counselor," I told him. "She said you failed me?"

"Um, let's see." He rifled through some papers and eyeballed one. "Clint Harp?" he said. I nodded. "Your test scores don't add up, son. And you didn't do the homework assignment, either." *Whoops.* "Yes, you failed. That's all there is to it."

In my heart, I knew I had not yet held up my end of the deal, especially since I had totally disregarded the *one* homework assignment, but I wasn't ready to accept defeat. I appealed to him to pass me now and promised to finish the work that was still due. "And I know there's the homework thing," I said, "but, I mean, this is just so hard."

Wrong choice of words.

"Clint, let me tell you what hard is," he shot back. "Surviving cancer is hard. And that's exactly what my wife and I once did. That's hard. You just didn't study."

"Yes, sir, I hear you, but you did say that if I—"

"Clint, you are an example of what I don't like about being a teacher," he cut in. "Get out of here and I'll let you know."

I leapt out of my seat, thanking him profusely as I bowed out of the doorway. I made a beeline straight to the campus chapel in the Tidwell Bible Building. I sat on a pew and whispered, "Lord, I'm not asking you to do magic here and make me pass. I'm just asking that you'll help me be okay with whatever's ahead."

As soon as I got home, the phone rang. It was my guidance counselor. "Clint, you passed the class," she said. "But one last thing—your professor wanted me to give you this message: 'Do your homework.'"

The next afternoon, still filled with relief, I slipped a manila envelope under my professor's door. It contained a handwritten note of gratitude and my completed final assignment. A few days later, with my family seated in the stands, I marched across the stage and received my diploma. *Phew.*

I'm glad things worked out the way they did, but in hindsight, there's no doubt I could've done so much better. I had much more to give, but back then, I really didn't know how. I only knew what it took to survive. That's what my childhood had taught me to do best. Survive.

*   *   *

I made it to Florida and began my first real full-time job. But as pumped as I was to be there doing work that I really loved and felt passionate about, during my first six months as area director of the youth ministry, every workday brought with it the same question: *How many more hours before I can talk to Kelly again?* Every night, we'd linger on the phone for hours at a time, and the next morning, I'd wander, bleary-eyed but blissful, into the office. Then by noon, I'd be eyeing the clock again, counting down to the next call with her.

St. Petersburg was brimming with old architecture and old people, and while the beaches were beautiful, it was often dreadfully hot. My early days were filled with recruiting volunteers, getting to know the students I'd be working with, connecting with the ministry's board members, and just getting the lay of the land. I made a couple of friends and was on my way. Setting up the ministry wasn't too difficult. As a volunteer in Waco, I'd learned from the best, so I just mirrored what I'd been taught.

That July, Kelly and I returned to her hometown of Tyler,

Texas, to say our vows, as our families made plans to join us for the big day.

*　　*　　*

The ceremony was beautiful, and we were lucky to be surrounded by so many people who loved us, but everything around it was a struggle. Suffice it to say that having all of our parents back in the same room for the first time in years was enough to create many moments of tension and emotion. And then in the middle of it all, my dad, with my stepmom, stepsister, nephew, and pregnant sister Bonnie in the back seat, got into a head-on collision. Thankfully, and most important, they and the other driver involved escaped death and serious injury, albeit narrowly. I found all this out just moments before the wedding rehearsal when I received a note from my aunt telling me that, though okay, my dad and family had been in an accident but that they wanted me to go ahead with the rehearsal. Kelly and I decided to trudge forward.

Later, after being released from the hospital, my family made it to the rehearsal dinner and we all basically limped our way through it. The next day the wedding went off without a hitch, and the following morning, Kelly and I boarded a plane to Mexico for our honeymoon. Given the whole insane ordeal, we joke that it's a miracle we ever returned.

Once we got back to the States, Kelly joined me in St. Petersburg. As we started our life together, far away from anyone we knew, the first reality of our marriage came into sharp focus: we were on our own. There would be no clear path, no set of rules, no master artist who would hand us The Grand Design. We were two young kids, figuring out how to live together and start a career in a new city. We had no clue what we were doing, but we did have each other. Together, we'd figure things out.

As much as we loved each other, the early months of married life came with challenges. Kelly and I are opinionated people. We both care how something looks, how something feels, how something smells. And we also experienced a lot of loss in the course of growing up, which can cause you to cling to what's most familiar, even if seemingly trivial. Early in life, I'd mastered the art of setting things up around me to work just how I needed them to. I had strong beliefs and an ability to hold on to them for dear life. But marriage is about letting go. Letting go of all the ways that *you* would do it and being open to how someone else might do it. I still struggle with it to this day, but marriage has whittled away at me in the best ways. I also happen to have chosen the best person to walk alongside me on that path. I realize that even more clearly now than I did during our first days of married life.

Kelly soon got a job at the Gap and I continued my work as an area director, even though it wasn't quite satisfying me like I thought it would. When a couple of my ministry's newest board members, Frank and Dawn, floated the idea of us moving to Europe with them to be part of a postmodern church plant once I was done with my current contract, we were incredibly excited. I wasn't even sure what a "postmodern church plant" involved, but if it meant living abroad with Kelly and doing ministry that we were passionate about, I was in. So we prayed and searched and talked and finally decided we wanted to go. Problem was, I made the mistake of sharing my plans of moving to Europe once my contract was up with my board.

A couple of months later, they let me go. To be fair, they had asked that we all be honest with one another about our plans and goals and how we were feeling about the ministry . . . okay, maybe I went a little too far a little too soon, but still.

It's weird to be a newlywed with an expensive college degree and no job. The precariousness of the situation really hit home when I landed the first job I could find cleaning toilets as a church janitor in the winter of 2002. For the record, janitors are great. Without them it would be a horrible, smelly world. But because I had more than $50,000 in college debt, being a janitor wasn't my plan. After janitorial life, my next job was as a junior high minister, which was basically the same gig: smelly, with a lot of messes to clean up. Being able to play the guitar and lead worship did come in handy, although by this time the fervor I'd had for a performance career had started to fade. I still loved music, and thought maybe one day I'd get back to it, but right then I needed to keep a little cash coming in. I started picking up handyman work, installing air-conditioning ducts, toilets, tile, crown molding, you name it.

That whole period was a test of our new marriage. Kelly and I were scared about money, and the way we argued reflected it. We were defensive, each trying to preserve those little bits, even the meaningless ones, of the life we'd dreamed of. We fought one hell of a battle over exactly how to put a new trash bag in the can. And one day we even had it out in the middle of the grocery store, in a scene I like to call "The Butter Offensive." We were checking off items from Kelly's thoughtfully made list when she said, "We need butter, Clint."

"I got this, Kelly."

"But, Clint, get the stick butter, okay?"

I was suddenly rankled. We argued for a bit until I finally laid out a proclamation. "Well, my mom has always just used tub butter even when baking," I announced, "but I guess we can just go ahead and have this luxury." Wrong choice of words.

Through angry tears, Kelly delivered the line I just might engrave on my tombstone: "A ninety-nine-cent luxury, Clint. Great!"

At the height of our financial anxiety, we also found ourselves excited about joining the church planting group. And no doubt it sounded better than sweaty twelve-hour days of caulking. But for me, a young guy filled with wanderlust, one sentence early on from our mission leaders Frank and Dawn sealed the deal: "You'll be living in Amsterdam and Paris." I was like, *Where do we sign?* Kelly and I were passionate about doing mission work and probably would have gone just about anywhere. But Paris? It felt like it couldn't really be true. They then explained that we'd have to raise our own support if we wanted to make it happen.

When it came to our decision to move to Europe, our friends were split in their opinions. Some advocated waiting until I'd paid down my student loans, and others supported the move as a great opportunity before we had kids. In the end, we made the choice to go, and we've never regretted it.

But first we needed to raise the money. In October 2002, we moved back to Texas to rally supporters. We figured it'd be easier to ask for funding in the state where Kelly had grown up and where we'd both attended college, and where several of our friends had settled. I got a part-time job as an account manager at a mortgage licensing firm in Dallas, which was ninety minutes west of Tyler. When my shift was done, I'd spend the rest of the day making calls and sending out support letters. Kelly was a nanny and taught home school for a local family.

On Sundays, we'd go around to churches and try to explain our mission. I wasn't a spiritual scholar, but I now understood what the postmodern movement was, in part, about: welcoming skeptics. Our new church would encourage congregants to question their faith and search for understanding. We'd be all about creating a community of searchers and allowing them the space to explore their own conceptions of God. No doubt this was some different theology than what we'd grown up with. And the fact that we were oftentimes asking for funding from mostly conservative Christians—those with some of the same traditional beliefs I'd been raised with, along with very little desire to learn too much about the postmodern Christian world—didn't make our path easy. On top of that, we weren't exactly going to some war-torn or third-world country with a desperate need. I'm sure a few of our listeners were trying to make sure we weren't just looking for a reason to move to Paris. But the truth was, we were genuinely excited about the ministry, and those we talked to could tell. For us, it seemed like the ultimate combination: doing meaningful work while also exploring a new world that seemed as fascinating to us as it did foreign. Many loving people reached into their pockets and helped make the way for us to go, and we will always be thankful for that.

Our initial goal was to raise $30,000, the minimum amount we'd need to live abroad for one year. We intended to stay for five. We hoped to gather enough seed money to fly to Amsterdam, begin working, and then take it one season at a time. With the exchange rate what it was in those days, we knew that even $30,000 was bare bones, but we believed in the mission so much, we were willing to survive on a tight budget.

By late spring of 2003, and after seven months of raising support, we were still short on committed funds. Very short. "Should we go and just try to make it work?" I said to Kelly. Neither of us was sure. But that's the gift of youth. With few precedents or set-in-stone rules, you can just step out, wide-eyed and hopeful, without overthinking things. A few weeks later, on a hot day in July, we boarded a plane to the Netherlands.

We make our blueprints. We dream our dreams. And even when our sketches are loosely rendered—or we haven't done all the homework—we end up someplace new. As Kelly and I would come to discover, rarely does that place match the one we envisioned. And yet for reasons that can seldom be predicted, we end up exactly where we ought to be.

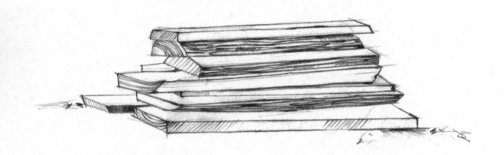

CHAPTER 5

Raw Materials

Raw materials are all around us. Whether at a store, in a lumberyard or dumpster, or still growing in the forest, the wood we need can be found. Once I've sketched out a design, I take the time to think through what kind of material I need. If, for instance, I'm building an outdoor table from teak, I'll call up my hardwood supplier and put in an order. If I'm building from reclaimed wood, I might go in search of some pallets or old barnwood. Those times when I can order exactly the wood I need, at the size I need it, are great, particularly when I'm on a deadline. But those times when I can work at my own pace and use what I have? That's when I find the work most fulfilling.

In the Netherlands, we moved into the top floor of a three-story house, crammed in a row of other homes just like it. To save on rent, we shared our two-bedroom quarters with a single American who coincidentally hailed from Dallas. Tight quarters, yes, but when you're as over the moon as we were to be doing our dream job, you hardly notice the squeeze. Our house was in The Hague, where the church plant ministry was headquartered. From there, we commuted to work in Amsterdam every day for three months to complete our mission training.

We loved The Hague, or Den Haag, as they call it there. For starters, the residents were among the friendliest people we'd ever met, and though Dutch was the official language, most of them spoke English, too. That eased our transition, big-time. Secondly, everyone rode bikes, and I do mean *everyone*. More bikes were parked outside the grocery store than cars. As summer and fall gave way to winter's freezing temperatures, Kelly and I, fresh from the Texas heat, were plenty cold. But pedaling around the city over bridges and along cobblestone paths lined with gorgeous tulips warmed us right up.

On our half-hour train commute into Amsterdam, I plowed through the seven books in the Chronicles of Narnia series by C. S. Lewis. Once in town, Kelly and I stood shivering, hands plunged deep in our pockets, waiting for a bus to take us to the church where we were interning. I'd wander over to a food truck to grab an *oliebollen*—a kind of dense doughnut just bigger than a golf ball, fried and covered in powdered sugar and served piping hot in a brown paper bag. One could last you an entire day, but by the time our bus approached, I'd easily thrown back a couple. Again, I tell you, I like to eat.

At the church, I was assigned to lead worship while Kelly's organizational skills were put toward managerial work. Ninety days and a ridiculous number of *oliebollens* later, our training was complete and we moved on to Paris. It was insane. I mean, who gets to live in a centuries-old apartment building, right smack in the middle of the city's 5th arrondissement, called the Latin Quarter, and steps away from where Ernest Hemingway once walked, as depicted in *A Moveable Feast*? Well, us. We lived just a ten-minute stroll from Notre-Dame, and Luxembourg Gardens, the famous tree-lined park with immaculate lawns, was practically our backyard. Our first days were devoted to learning French (*Je suis désolée, je ne parle pas français*—"I'm sorry, I don't speak French"—is all I have to show now, years after those courses) and working with our team to found this thing we called a church community. On the side, I began training for the Paris Marathon, which felt like coming back to my roots; though I'd continued to run since college, it had been five years since my last race. After the marathons I completed as a freshman and then a junior at Baylor, Paris would be my third.

Soon after moving in, we decided to paint our apartment. It was a fun time, as we were really getting our first chance at making our place our own with a little paint and sweat. "For the kitchen, how about a deep, rich chocolate brown to match the mint green tiles?" suggested Kelly, embracing the bold. Sounded wild to me, and I had my doubts, but we went with it. For the other two rooms, we agreed on something in the neighborhood of a pale yellow. The next morning, we rode the metro to a home improvement store and struggled back onto the train hauling five-gallon buckets of paint. Kelly was exactly right, and the kitchen color turned out great, but the living room and bedroom walls were a disaster. Two different but equally horrible shades of yellow later, we finally settled on khaki. With the aroma of fresh paint still in the air, the IKEA furniture we'd ordered arrived. Box upon box filled our apartment, and I got to work constructing our bed, armoire, chairs, and tables with an L-shaped Allen wrench the size of my pinkie. This was our new home.

By the time we arrived in Paris, the lid on my own personal spiritual rigidity had already been loosened. Thanks to Kelly, and a handful of eye-opening experiences, I was now amenable to stepping further outside my adherence to the stricter conservative Christian practices. (A quick note before I dive in: I'm making no universal judgments here. What one person believes is totally up to him or her. While I was growing away from many of the things I was taught in my younger years, I understand that many people still hold tightly to those beliefs. And that is their prerogative. For me, it all boils down to holding whatever beliefs we have with a gentle love, allowing for the reality that ours might not be for everyone, and remaining open to and accepting of those we differ with.)

Now where were we? Oh yes, that's right . . . back home in the Bible Belt. There, things were, well, a bit stricter than they were in Europe. Let's put it this way: at home, no cussing; no drinking; no smoking; and, for crying out loud, people keep their clothes on! In Europe, as we were quickly learning, everyone seemed to be smoking, it was borderline rude to refuse a drink, and people said the word *shit* the way we say *shoot*. And when it came to the human body, nakedness didn't really shock anybody there. On magazine covers and billboards and beaches, in TV ads and shop windows, bare skin was unabashedly on display. Quite honestly, it was like background noise; because it was so out there, no one seemed to care. At first, given my conservative rearing, I found all of it a little shocking. But the more time I spent in this culture, opening my mind to the way other people see the world, the more I found myself accepting and loving others regardless of their lifestyles or differences. I'd never make an argument for rampant nudity in the world (let's be honest, there are just so few of us, myself included, who ever can or even want to be showing off any of that!), and you'll probably never catch me with a cigarette in my mouth (mainly because I have a weird thing about certain aromas and personally smelling good, but who cares about that). But I did start to see things from a new perspective.

And then there was the reason we were in Paris in the first place: to plant a postmodern church community. Our team pastor, Frank, and his wife, Dawn, who were married with three children, lived in the apartment right below ours; the loose plan was for Kelly and me to essentially be their lieutenants. We all thought that, armed with our enthusiasm and a bit of an edgier brand of Christianity, we'd have a decent shot at sparking a movement. The trouble was, we couldn't even strike the first match. Our premise: the French were hungry for a spiritual awakening. The reality: the average Parisian we approached didn't care as much about church as they did about just basic human connection and relationships. Can you blame them? We managed to organize a few parties for locals in Frank and Dawn's apartment (we had no church building) and made connections with people who did seem to be in need of a community. But other than that, it was really slow going.

We did, however, get one thing right. "Have any of you heard about the church just off the Champs-Élysées that feeds homeless people?" Dawn asked at one of our team meetings. I hadn't. But desperate to make some kind of tangible contribution, and realizing that Paris was filled with homeless people, Kelly and I went to investigate. There, we met the leaders of another ministry that served meals to anyone who dropped by. From then on, one day each week, Kelly and I, often with at least one or two of our fellow team members, joined the soup kitchen crew. Walking into the hundred-year-old kitchen housed in the church basement was like stepping back in time. We'd throw pans onto the old cast-iron gas stoves and brown the meat for a spaghetti lunch. Once, when the bottom of my pan got coated with burnt meat and gristle, I thought I'd screwed up. "Just pour some wine into the hot pan," a Frenchwoman told me. And voilà, that's how I learned the art of deglazing, which I use to this day. During our entire stay in Paris, our church-plant team cooked in that soup kitchen. And long after we'd left the city, our team continued to volunteer there.

When we weren't at the soup kitchen or spending our daytime hours in language classes, we were trying to get Parisians interested in our mission. Our nights were spent either trying to stay warm in our apartment, or occasionally going out to a movie and dinner with new friends and fellow team members. Despite the fact that, in the time Kelly and I were there, we never managed to get more than a trickle of folks interested in our church, life was certainly never dull. That's because whatever was or was not happening with the ministry, it was all playing out against the backdrop of this amazing City of Light. The thing is, paradise was quite expensive. During our first three months abroad, with an incredibly high rent payment and costs of commuting back and forth to Amsterdam, we blew through $12,000 of the $30,000 we'd raised. By the time we got to Paris we were limping at best.

*   *   *

Before Kelly and I had left the States for Europe, my grandmother Martin, Mom's mom, had fallen ill. I'd visited her before our departure, knowing it might be the last time I'd see her. One month after we arrived in the Netherlands, Kelly and I went on a mandatory retreat out in the country. After a walk with some colleagues and friends, we returned to the hotel to find a note for me at the front desk. "Call your mother," it read. *My grandmother has passed*, I thought as I tapped out my mother's number.

"Hi, Mom," I said when she picked up. "What's going on?"

She paused. "Honey," she finally said, "your grandmother Harp died." The night before, Mom told me, my father's mother had prepared herself for bed as usual, brushing her teeth under the watchful eye of the Clark Gable poster she'd bought on a trip to Universal Studios that she and I once took together. She'd climbed into bed, said her prayers, and drifted off to sleep. She never woke up.

Losing a loved one is never easy, but this was a complete shock. I'd been expecting to lose Grandmother Martin, which was hard enough, but my father's mother? I was stunned and devastated. I made my way into the woods alone and cried. That afternoon, I lay on my bed and listened to a hymn that my old friend Chris once wrote. "And with your final heartbeat / Kiss the world good-bye," went the lyrics. "Then go in peace, and laugh on Glory's side." I must've replayed that song thirty times on my old-school MP3 player.

A few months later, after settling into our Paris apartment. I got another call from home. "What's up?" I said, my pulse quickening when I heard my mother's distressed voice.

"Honey," she said, "Mama's gone on home." Mama, of course, was Grandmom Martin, my mother's mom.

I couldn't travel back home for either of my grandmothers' funerals. Kelly and I had no money for that, nor did our families. So across an ocean, with nothing to do on the day of Ann Callaway Martin's funeral but put together IKEA furniture and go for a run, and with a whole lot of sadness, I said good-bye. There are times when we're called on to rise up and meet whatever life sends our way, to make the best of an impossible situation. And then there are those seasons when, miles away from anything familiar, all we can do is be raw.

*　*　*

By the time Kelly and I decided to become part of church planting, I'd moved away from some of what I'd been taught as a child. Not all of it, of course: I did and still do respect many of the principles I was raised with. But a few things needed to shift, and really, I suppose that's what it means to grow up—to grow into what principles and faith mean to you. For instance, I'd grown up thinking I needed to have an answer to every spiritual question that arose. "I don't really know" was not an acceptable response in many of the circles I grew up in. But within our ministry team in Paris, not only was it all right to admit "I don't know," we actively encouraged one another to explore God's mysteries. The more I did that, the more the rigid religious walls I'd built in childhood began crumbling.

Like my take on drinking: back in Atlanta when I was sixteen, my church had welcomed a new pastor, who'd rolled into town from Waco, of all places. He wanted to shake things up, and boy, did he. In place of old hymnals, we sang new worship songs, with the words projected up onto a screen at the front of the sanctuary. *Look out!* He also brought in a band with guitar and drums. All good. And then he crossed a line.

There's a Bible verse that says deacons shouldn't be "given to too much wine." Our church took that to the extreme, falling in with the Southern Baptist tradition that deacons should not drink at all. Period. Well, our new pastor suggested that we change that rule and allow deacons to pour up a glass now and then. I didn't like it one bit. At the time, I was living with my family in an apartment building flanked by two halfway houses. My parents would sometimes invite the men from those houses into our home for Bible study. From my spot on the couch, I'd listen to their stories. Their addiction to alcohol had cost them so much.

Not that I'd never had a drink. One evening when I was twelve, I was hanging with some of my cousins at the Roost. After the grown-ups went off to bed, one of my cousins mixed up some vodka and orange juice to make herself a screwdriver. "Want a taste?" she asked. I nodded, desperately wanting to impress her and feel cool.

She put the rim of the glass to my lips and I took a swig. It tasted like hair spray. But it piqued my curiosity enough. I grabbed a Miller Lite from the fridge and downed it like chocolate milk. Just as I was guzzling the final suds, I heard heavy footsteps on the stairs. It had to be my uncle Howard. I threw out the beer can, quickly grabbed a Diet Coke from the fridge, and knocked it back in an attempt to hide the odor. "Hey, buddy," my uncle said when he rounded the corner into the kitchen. "You're still up?" I nodded and rushed off, hoping he wouldn't notice the smell of my breath. Ten minutes later I was passed out on the couch like an old drunk. I didn't touch the stuff again for over a decade.

By the time the new pastor proposed relaxing the church's alcohol rules, I knew where I stood: arm in arm with the teetotalers of the world. The congregational leaders decided to hold a town hall meeting one Sunday night, so church members could vote on whether deacons should be allowed to drink. Before the vote, long lines of people made their way up to microphones to argue for or against the issue. Usually, Sunday evening services were poorly attended, but on the night of the vino vote, you would've thought Jesus Himself was the guest speaker. The place was packed.

Soon it was my turn at the mic. "None of the men I've met from halfway houses set out to be alcoholics and lose everything," I said, with that brand of earnest conviction reserved only for adolescence. "It all started with one sip." My tears began to flow. "My own grandfather had a tendency to drink," I went on, "and it has been really tough on our family." (I recalled, but didn't share, that Granddad Martin used to ask me, "If we aren't supposed to drink, then why would Jesus turn water into wine?" I usually replied, "That was more like juice, Granddad. It's different from our wine today.") *Smart aleck.*

My heartfelt plea in church that evening drew some "Amens," and a few people were even dabbing at their eyes. But none of that mattered in the end, because we lost the vote. I was like, *Whatever. Go wild, deacons. Go wild.*

Fast-forward to 2002 in St. Petersburg, Florida, when Kelly and I first met the leaders of our church planting organization. They all ordered a beer for lunch. I didn't follow suit. But weeks later, at the home of a couple who hosted us as part of our pre-trip orientation, the group shared a bottle of wine. This time, I decided to partake. *Hair spray.*

Nowadays I love a spicy margarita, a nice Cabernet, or a strong IPA, but that's neither here nor there. The point is that, once again, the narrow-mindedness of my youth was starting to come loose. I was an uptight and inflexible guy who needed to have my boundaries expanded, who needed to understand that there's more than one right way to do life. In Europe, I realized just how little I knew, and that the capital T in "Truth" sometimes comes in shades of gray and leaves a lot of room for interpretation. I did not and do not have all the answers, and in Paris, I finally stopped pretending I did. Life, I was discovering, was so much bigger than one set of rules.

* * *

Coming up on a year into our time in Paris, we were running out of money, fast. I get it that Jesus once multiplied five loaves and two fishes to feed a multitude on the banks of the river, but maybe sometimes we're meant to learn the lessons of going hungry. I mean, we still ate. But when you're constantly worried that your next subway fare might be your last, you're awfully close to the edge and it's exhausting.

Enter the IRS. We'd filed for an extension to complete our taxes, and in May, we were finally ready for the task. This was the first time for us to file separate from an employer, so we were in uncharted waters. Up to this point, I'd always gotten a refund, so when our tax preparer pushed the "calculate" button at the end of our online tax form, my jaw hit the floor. "You owe $6,000," it read. *What?!* Throw in the $4,000 in credit card bills we'd amassed to keep the lights and water on, and you can see why we were up to our eyeballs in debt.

Turns out that as missionaries, we were officially considered self-employed, which meant we were responsible for estimating and paying our own taxes directly to the IRS every quarter. I remember our organization saying something about that, but we were candidly on our own, and left to my devices back then, let's just say you wouldn't have wanted me to manage your finances. When you work for a US employer, your company typically withholds a portion of your Social Security and Medicare taxes from your paychecks automatically. Not so when you're an entrepreneur, or in our case, missionaries living abroad. We'd set aside some money to square up at year's end, but it wasn't nearly enough. We didn't even have the money to cover our monthly bills in the first place. We were screwed.

You'd think that as a business major at Baylor, I might've picked up a few pointers on handling finances—maybe I should've studied a bit more. But I was used to a more "fly by the seat of your pants" existence, and quite frankly, that method had been working okay so far in my young adulthood. But not in Paris. Not when my wife and I were in a foreign country with no safety net, no family money to back us up, and no generous supporter to bankroll our spiritual mission and pull us out of our $10,000 hole.

Over the next few days, Kelly and I had many long talks. The toughest one came late one evening in the shadows of our living room.

"I'm the reason for our financial situation, Kelly," I told her.

"Why do you say that?" she asked.

"Because I don't know how to manage money," I admitted. "I never have. I knew that, but I didn't want to address it. But now there's no escaping it."

Life has its patterns. The sun comes up and then it goes down. You can count on that every single day. And then there are those personal patterns, good and bad, we learn early on and keep living out, like: if I'm genuinely nice to this person, there's a high likelihood my kindness will be returned. Or, if I don't change my oil until the engine light comes on, I'll have to spend hundreds in repairs. Back then, one of my most regrettable patterns, a habit that had stuck with me like gum on a shoe, was to ignore financial realities until my hand was forced—and then hope somebody with money would offer me a "get out of jail free" card. I basically lived to enjoy each moment, with little worry for how I'd later settle the check. Knowing it was time to end this pattern, Kelly and I made a difficult choice: we would cut our mission trip short by four years and go home. Even before our team leader had the chance to try to talk us out of it, we had purchased our return flights. That's how sure I was that I needed to break the cycle of expecting someone to save my behind.

Our ministry team was disappointed. Many of them were also struggling financially, yet somehow they were working things out. "Isn't there some way you can stay?" Frank asked me. We didn't budge. Then another married couple on our team offered to cover our tax bill. It was incredibly generous of them and Kelly and I were so thankful, but I was finally clear that their proposal was tantamount to dangling crack in the face of a hard-core addict. For me, it wasn't about getting bailed out one more time. It was about growing up. We wanted to repay our own debt. We politely declined their offer.

While money was the reason we had to come home early, things were also turning out different than we'd imagined with the ministry. We were starting to have some major doubts and didn't feel like we had a lot of reasons to fight to stay. Why had we felt the need to plant a church in a place where the congregations and culture were older than the country we came from? The idea of continuing to befriend locals, always hoping that we could eventually reel them into this postmodern church concept, left me feeling conflicted. I personally wasn't convinced of the spiritual value of our mission anymore. But regardless, we were broke, and it was time for us to go.

Our last team meeting was painful. Tears were shed. Some people expressed feeling abandoned, while others just stayed quiet. "We know you're doing what you feel like you have to do," one teammate said, "and we wish you well." But the predominant feeling in the room was one of sadness. When we returned to our apartment that evening, my wife and I just sat together and cried.

It was raining the day we left Paris. The team members who could came to say good-bye. They gathered outside of our building, in the rain, and helped us load up everything we owned into the back of the taxi van that would take us to the train station. Our friend Christian's girlfriend, Nadine, cracked an inside joke her family loved: "I wish I never knew you," she quipped, a smile on her face. That joke felt awkward to most everyone except me—I'm a sucker for dry humor and loved her attempt to lighten the mood. Later, Kelly and I stood at the back of the train with all our belongings piled around us. A young woman walked into our train car. And though it's rare in Paris to talk to strangers, and even more rare to find one who speaks fluent English, we struck up a conversation.

"What do you do for a living?" I asked her at one point. Without hesitation, she said, "I'm a stripper." She told us she'd danced in clubs all around Europe for years. It struck me that before moving to Europe, I'd have blushed at her story, and I'd no doubt have judged her severely. But in a train car that was carrying us away from an experience that had clearly changed me, I enjoyed meeting and talking with her. She was no different from me. She was

God's child, just as Kelly and I were. And for the duration of that ride, we were all traveling alongside one another on the same road.

Later, Kelly and I would reflect that our time abroad hadn't gone anything like we'd planned. We'd hoped to master the French language, crisscross the continent, help start a flourishing church community, and maybe even have our first child while living in Europe. Instead, we were leaving with hardly enough French under our belts to hold a conversation with a five-year-old, and the pages in our passports were woefully unstamped. Though I knew we had made the right decision, a feeling of failure hung over me.

If I'd known then what was just up the road and around the bend for Kelly and me, I would've left the City of Light without a single regret. But in the cloud of disappointment that surrounded our departure, it would be a while before I realized that Paris had given us exactly what we needed—the raw materials with which to build a life.

PART TWO

CRAFTSMAN

Creativity is allowing yourself to make mistakes. Art is knowing which ones to keep.

—Scott Adams, cartoonist

CHAPTER 6

Wood Grain

Looking at a pile of wood sitting on my shop floor might be one of my favorite things to do. I've built enough tables to know that what might appear to be a mess in front of me is really a beautiful creation just waiting to be put together. The pieces are there. It just comes down to sorting them out. I lay each board, one at a time, on the ground. If the wood could speak, it might be annoyed with my indecision and pickiness while I toe-kick and bump each board together. From there, I can step back and see how it might all eventually fit.

"Babe, I saw this little white house today," Kelly told me one evening back in Dallas. "Pretty small, but so stinkin' cute."

"Where is it?"

"It's over on Ross Ave. Want to go see it?"

"Yeah, okay, sure," I said. I figured it was free to look.

We'd been back in the States for a year by then, and what a whirlwind twelve months it had been. Even before we left France, I'd called my old boss at the mortgage licensing firm and asked if I could have my old job back. There happened to be a vacancy, and he agreed. Meanwhile, Kelly applied for a job as a sixth-grade teacher and was hired. When we touched down in Dallas in the summer of 2004, she had just a few weeks to prep for the coming school year, and I had one week to get settled before heading back to work.

We stayed with friends at first. Then a couple of other friends left town for a few weeks and offered us their place. We also had to borrow friends' cars here and there, as we were without wheels. Neither Kelly nor I had ever bought a vehicle, but after working a few months, we scraped together our nickels for a minuscule down payment on an incredibly cheap and incredibly used Honda Civic. It even came with a cigarette hole burned in the driver's seat. We bought it with our own hard-earned money, and we loved it. It was as perfect as it was purple. Kelly made her way through Dallas traffic every day in what sounded like a sewing machine on wheels. As for me, I rode my bike, which I loved. It reminded me of our time in Amsterdam, when our Euro adventure was still shiny and new— plus, I didn't have to spend on gas. I'd roll into work a bit early so the sweat on my forehead could dry before my coworkers arrived.

Soon after we settled into our jobs, we rented a little two-bedroom apartment down the road from some friends. The place was, frankly, a pit stop, nice enough for the time being but not so much for the long term. We settled in and began paying off that tax bill and more of my student loans. We even managed to save a bit and began daydreaming about eventually buying a home. Years earlier, when Kelly had had the privilege of meeting my grandmother Harp for the first time, my grandmom had broken out the family albums. In one black-and-white photo from Donald and Camille's first year of marriage, they sat on the front of their house holding paintbrushes. That photo, which we always remembered, brought us new inspiration for our lives ahead. We wanted to be them.

When Kelly mentioned that white house on Ross Avenue and we drove by to see it, I was unimpressed. The neighborhood was an eclectic gathering of homes, very random and worn. Some yards looked cared for, but others were brown and overgrown with weeds. It was the kind of street where you'd see someone strutting around in a fringed vest and bare feet holding a baby wearing nothing but a cloth diaper. Very bohemian. Not that there was anything wrong with that, but it wasn't what I had in mind. Paris had changed me and I'd returned home a much more cultured person than I was before, but this was a bridge too far. We were back in Texas again. Adventure over, man.

The 1940s cottage was as charming of a fixer-upper as Kelly had told me it was, or at least it appeared that way from the exterior, but that was a moot point since I wasn't sold on the neighborhood.

Kelly persisted. "It could be really cute!" she kept saying. "The outside isn't that bad, and maybe it won't need too much work on the inside. Besides, it's all we can afford if we don't want to move to the suburbs. And this neighborhood is a good investment." I couldn't see it at the time, but Kelly was right. The neighborhood was growing with new restaurants and renovations, and it was clear people were buying in.

At the time, the country was in a housing boom, and I spent my days helping people lock down mortgage brokers and lenders licenses. To be honest, when I'd first started that job, I hadn't truly known what a mortgage was. My boss had to explain it to me. You can imagine how that must have inspired confidence. But it was the knowledge I'd gleaned from that job that had planted the seed of possibility of home ownership in the heart and mind of a lifelong renter. Maybe one day we could indeed be like my grandparents and own our own house. I just wasn't as sure as my wife that *this* should be our first rodeo. But Kelly seemed so dang passionate about it, I relented. "I really don't love the neighborhood," I told her a few days into her campaign, "but if you think it's a good idea, then let's call the Realtor."

Kelly was fearless. Her absolute confidence that we could buy and renovate this home bolstered my own. She was excited and ready to rip into the project. We just had to figure out how we'd pay for it.

The following week, the Realtor walked us through the house—all 968 square feet of it, with popcorn ceilings throughout. The place looked like it had last been remodeled in the 1960s. The previous owner had already moved out and left the house clean, but it was in desperate need of an update. In the backyard, an outdoor shed was home to the washer and dryer; not ideal, but we could live with it. And on the outside of the house was a giant satellite dish sitting atop a large pole cemented into the ground that seemed big enough to contact life-forms on other planets. If we looked past all that, the place was a darling two-bedroom, one-bath. The asking price was $150,000. My confidence started brewing, and I suddenly felt like I could learn whatever I needed to in order to make that house right.

"Clint, let's offer a hundred thousand," Kelly suggested. Though she'd never owned property herself, her parents had bought and sold several homes, and that gave her the self-assurance that I, a bidding rookie, lacked.

"What?" I said. "That's over thirty percent off the asking price!"

"Have you seen what we're going to have to do to it?" she shot back.

I paused, recalling the popcorn ceilings and outdated interior. "Good point," I said. "Okay, but I really hope we don't piss the seller off."

I'll never know if the guy was ticked, because we had no contact with him. But through our agents, we eventually settled on a purchase price of $120,000. And because we were right smack in the middle of a housing boom, the bank didn't require us to put any money down. In fact, the seller even covered our closing costs. I still don't know how it all worked out, but it did. And in July

2005, a little over a year after our European misadventure ended, Kelly and I were packing up to move into our first home. The kid with the big head, tight red sweatpants, and buckteeth was finally getting somewhere.

Moving day arrived. A buddy and I strapped down a hutch I'd purchased at an estate sale, securing it with ties to the back of our borrowed pickup truck. When I got to the house, we began unloading the hutch. "Hey, Blake," I said, "did you already grab the two small drawers that were here on the top?

"Nope, I don't think so," he told me.

"Huh, that's weird," I said. "Maybe they're still back at the apartment."

But they weren't. When I retraced my path, I found them on the side of the road, in tatters, right at the spot where I'd thought I heard something fall but was too tired to stop and investigate. I've moved over thirty times in my life and have rarely broken anything. Those smashed drawers were my first major casualties, and it stung. We'd keep that hutch with the missing drawers for the next six years. "One day," I kept saying, "I'll build new drawers to match." Never did.

I don't know what excited me more: purchasing the house, or knowing I'd get to buy some tools to remodel the place. In all the gifts we received at our wedding, there wasn't a single hammer, screwdriver, or wrench. I'd always been jealous of guys who were given "tool showers" before they tied the knot, and now I had a chance to remedy things. We came up with a modest budget of $5,000 for the whole house remodel, the limit on our credit card and an amount we knew we could pay off. I bought a budget-friendly combo pack of battery-powered tools, a hammer, and a few other must-haves. "Kelly, come look at these!" I announced as soon as I got home. I beamed as I showed her the set.

It was scary to max out our credit card again, but we figured we were saving such a huge amount on renovations doing them ourselves that it would be worth it. We scraped the popcorn off the ceilings; installed a new countertop; painted the interior; closed off an internal door that had no use; and hung, taped, and mudded a lot of drywall. We also completely overhauled the bathroom, which wasn't part of the original plan. But Kelly came home one day and found me in the middle of it, gutting the whole thing. The small bathroom was covered in cedar planks that we thought we'd paint, but I pulled one board down to see what was behind it, and then the next thing you know, I'd pulled everything down. My bad! With the help of a friend, and using the skills I'd picked up as a handyman in St. Pete, as well as a few nuggets I'd learned from Granddad Martin, we made that thing happen. Kelly tiled the entire shower herself. I can still see her sitting on the edge of the new tub covered in grout, with her hair pulled back, wearing a long-sleeved Baylor T-shirt and feeling so proud of what we were doing. We gave that little house every bit of love we could muster. Even our friends came over and threw in some effort. It was a rich time.

*   *   *

We actually stopped going to church when we got back from Europe. Church was the reason we'd moved abroad, but church was the last place we wanted to be when we returned. It's not that we'd given up on our faith. But our year of trying to launch a new congregation had been so intense, we just craved a hiatus to catch our breath. This was the first time in my life I hadn't attended services, which is probably why it initially felt strange not to go.

One Sunday morning when we were at home, probably doing

some work on the house, the phone rang. It was Meredith, Kelly's childhood friend from Tyler.

"Kelly," she said without pause, "Kyle died this morning at church. He's dead."

Kyle, who'd grown up in Kelly's hometown and was beloved by everyone, was the same Kyle who had made me want to go to Baylor. The guy who had once made an awkward kid from Georgia feel comfortable and welcome was gone. After I met him, Kyle eventually became the pastor at Waco's University Baptist Church, a congregation of misfits, doubters, and outliers. Everyone knew and loved him. On that Sunday morning, Meredith explained to Kelly through tears, Kyle had climbed into the baptismal pool to baptize a young girl. Realizing that the congregation couldn't hear him, he reached out to adjust a microphone that was set up just in front of the pool. No one knew that the water Kyle was standing in had a current running through it due to a mistake in the electrical grounding. Within moments, Kyle was gone.

Late that afternoon, my heart heavy with sorrow, I went out to a tennis court by myself. I took six balls and served them, one by one, across the court. After serving all six, I'd walk to the other side of the net, gather up the balls, and serve them all again. I did that over and over and over until the sun set. I felt like I'd been socked in the gut. One minute, Kyle had been helping a young woman take the next step on her own personal faith journey. The next, he was taking his final breath.

Kyle and his congregation had been among those who'd supported us financially in Europe. Not only had he been a friend, but he'd also gone out of his way to help us raise money for our dream. On the day we all lost him, he'd been planning to give a sermon that he had no doubt spent some time preparing. It was all about loving God, building something beautiful during our days here on earth, and living life to the fullest. The content of that sermon, which existed in the form of notes found later in his Bible, eventually became the church's guiding principles and motto "Love God, embrace beauty, and live life to the fullest." And in the years to come, as Kelly and I fumbled our way forward, trying to figure out what to do next, I also made it my own: *#lovebuildrun*.

Life is messy. It comes with bumps, bruises, and uneven surfaces. Like wood, you can't predict its grain or its texture, or how it'll all eventually fit together. What Kyle left for me and so many others was a legacy: embrace the mess. Let your kids roll all over you on the living room floor. Let the dishes go undone for now and spend the time connecting with the people you love. If you have to wallow in the mud, really jump in. And if you're going to live on planet Earth, then do it, and do it well. It's all just part of the madness and unpredictability of life, and we should enjoy it while we have it.

* * *

When it came to living life to the fullest, I can't say Kelly and I were actually doing so in our jobs, but we were thankful to have work that covered our expenses and to be making a dent in our debt. That reality began to shift as we sunk more and more cash into our fixer-upper. While we could cover all our bases, things were definitely tight, and I liked the idea of finding a job with a higher ceiling. It was time for me to go in search of greener pastures.

The father-in-law of a friend of mine owned a company that sold copy machines around Dallas. I decided to reach out, and got set up with an interview. I hated the idea of a sales job, and making cold calls in particular sounded like the Fifth Circle of Hell, but we needed more cash than I was bringing in. "We'd love to hire you to work here as a salesman. When can you start?" I was asked by my eventual manager who interviewed me. "Amazing, I'll put in my two weeks notice," I heard myself say.

I hated it from day one. It was a wonderful company with great people . . . but I wasn't cut out for it.

I tried to make the most of the job, really I did. I walked into and out of every place that might possibly need a copier or a printer. Day after day, I'd drive around the city, trying to make a sale to any creature with breath. The answer was almost always no, and more often than not, it came with a distant stare that spoke volumes: *Shoo, fly. I can't be bothered.* It was a lonely existence that left me feeling defeated and worn out. But through it all there was one thing that kept me going: building furniture.

Back when we first returned to Dallas and were still in the two-bedroom "place holder" apartment, I'd taken on my first ever furniture project. My friend Jordan and his wife, Christy, had a family table they wanted to fix up. I'd mentioned to Jordan that I wanted to try my hand at bringing old furniture back to life. He was into it.

"Here you go, Clint," Jordan told me one day. "Take this antique family heirloom of ours and do your thing!"

"Are you sure?" I asked.

"Yeah, you bet. Have fun!" I loved that he was so willing to give me a chance.

I got after it. In the evening and on weekends for a whole month, I stripped that table down. After removing all the old varnish, I attempted to stain it. Not knowing anything about stain and paying little attention to the instructions, I did everything wrong. Not only did I brush it on real thick without wiping it off, I did it all indoors. Our upstairs neighbor, suffocating from the fumes, was at our door moments later, asking what in the world we were up to. I finally finished the project and took it back to my friends. They loved it. They also wouldn't have told me if they hated it. My next project was an antique Jenny Lind bed from Kelly's mom. Filled with turnings, it was incredibly difficult to strip. Thankfully, because I was planning to paint it, not *every* bit of old paint or stain had to be removed. That one turned out really nice, and I was hungry for more.

By "more," I don't mean more refinishing, though. Frankly, as satisfying as those first two restoration projects had been, and as much as I'd loved losing myself in the process for hours, it wasn't enough. I had this nagging sense of wanting to actually build something from scratch—to create furniture of my own.

So on the weekends, when I wasn't selling copiers, I went to work on the back patio of our first house on Ross Ave. First, I dusted off the few tools I'd bought for our home remodel: a miter saw (aka chop saw), a circular saw, and a battery-powered drill. One day I woke up and just decided to make two tall green desks (I was really into this "working while standing" kick at the time). The legs, which I assembled using 2x4s, had hand-cut tapers. I also sawed a hole in the skirt of each table to make room for a drawer, although just as I never got around to replacing the drawers missing from the hutch, I never made those drawers, either. I nailed the whole thing together with roofing nails, and though the tables were a bit wobbly, they looked really cool and Kelly loved them. I now wanted to go bigger.

Our little house, in the way of closets, had one in the entryway and a small one off the living room, but that was it. I remembered how the old apartments in Paris seldom had closets, so most everyone used armoires. I decided Kelly should have one, too. I set out to make her both an armoire and a dining table.

With only two basic skinny desks in my portfolio, I was a total rookie. I figured that if a table was slats, a skirt, and legs, then an armoire must be a box with doors. I ran to the store, picked up some pine, and brought it home like a proud puppy with a squirrel in its mouth. I set everything up on our back patio and threw a tarp on it each evening to protect it from any rain. The end products were rudimentary at best, but Kelly adored them. And I was hooked. I had no doubt that I'd build more furniture. The only question was when.

A few weeks later, Kelly and I visited my granddad Martin. He was living in North Georgia, in the mountain house he'd built by hand. When we walked in, he was sitting by the window, just as I remembered him doing at the Roost. I was eager to show him my creations, so I'd brought some pictures with me. I handed him the photos. He studied the images for a long moment, glanced at me, looked back at my work, looked back at me, and then finally gave me his stamp of approval, Martin-style:

"Well," he said, "you're not a dumbass!"

Seriously, from him that was like "I love you."

Later that night, he called me at my mom's place.

"Hey, cowboy," he said. "When are you leaving town?"

"Day after tomorrow," I told him. "Need some help with something?"

"Just come by the house tomorrow morning?" he said.

"Yes, sir," I said. "See you tomorrow."

I arose early the next day and traveled solo to my granddad's house. Again, I found him sitting by the window.

"What did you use to build that stuff?" he asked.

"Well," I said, "I've got a chop saw, a circular saw, and a drill."

"Do you have a table saw?"

"No, sir."

"Do you have a drill press?"

"I do not."

"Well then, what the hell else do you have?" he pressed.

"Well, Granddad, that's it, really. Those three tools. Oh, and a hammer."

"And you really liked building those pieces?"

I nodded.

"Well then," he said, "you're going to need some more tools. I'll give you some money to go and buy yourself some. Get a pencil. I'll tell you what you need. Then you go back home and research how much it'll be and give me a price." I was blown away.

It was just the boost I needed. I jotted down the tools he mentioned: A table saw. A drill press. A hand planer. Some chisels. A dado blade for my table saw. "You know what a dado blade is?" he asked. I didn't. "You can cut tongue-and-groove joints with it and a bunch of other stuff. Get it. Okay?"

As we drove home to Dallas later that week, I dreamed the whole ride about one thing: building furniture. My grandfather was willing to invest in my tools, which meant I'd have everything I needed to really develop my craft. "Could I somehow build furniture full-time?" I wondered aloud to Kelly. How cool would it be to set up some kind of furniture business? The two of us talked for hours about the possibilities, and by the time we pulled into our driveway, I was sure this was my new path. There was only one thing standing in my way: my job as a copier salesman.

During my lunch breaks, I swung over to Home Depot and priced out the tools my granddad had asked me to look for; then I sent him the grand total. Though I was overwhelmed with work for the next few months, my desire to build furniture never dimmed. Little by little, I began prepping. I'd need a real shop. That meant I'd have to finally repair our garage floor, which looked like it had withstood a major earthquake. Until you have to break up a cement floor on your own with a sledgehammer, two hundred square feet doesn't seem very big. But I got it done. Over two days, to save money, I beat the crap out of that cement and cleared it out so a concrete company could pour a new slab. I got rid of the old concrete

Shawshank Redemption–style, throwing out a few pieces at a time in the garbage each week. It was months before the pile was all gone.

Not long after I overhauled the garage, Granddad's check for $1,250 arrived in the mail. A few days later I was at Home Depot having my own tool shower, thrown by Verner. I've had many great moments so far in life, but a truly special one was setting up that garage with all those woodworking tools.

No, I didn't know what I was doing, and in a way, I still don't. But I did have a sense of what it took to build something from scratch. My grandfather had shown me that. When he was building the new Roost up in the mountains of Dahlonega, Georgia, I watched him as he and his workers took a chainsaw and cut out notches in giant beams so they would fit together. Years later, I'd take on projects that called for some interesting joinery and details, and that's when my granddad would come to mind. He mostly used the tried-and-true approach—basically, he just tinkered around as long as necessary until he could figure out how to construct something solid—and that stayed with me. Through trial and error, you just have to stick with it. It might take a little longer to build something lasting and beautiful, I've learned, but it is well worth the effort.

I kept going to my day job, and I must've been doing something right because I had managed to land two big clients that would eventually be among the company's most lucrative accounts. Trouble was, I was miserable. Maybe I should've tried to figure out a way to balance rewarding work at night in the garage with unfulfilling work during the day, but I couldn't escape the sense that I needed to get out. It just didn't feel right. And after three months, I chose to follow that feeling—I quit.

On my last day, the owner's son called me into his office.

"So you're leaving," he said from behind his desk. "Clint, are you sure?"

"I've been so thankful for the opportunity," I said. "But, yes, I'm sure."

"What are you going to do?"

"I'm going to build furniture."

He stared at me. "Furniture?"

"Yes," I said confidently. "Furniture."

"Do you have clients lined up?" he pressed, out of a genuine feeling of concern, as he truly was such a nice person.

I told him I didn't. "I know it sounds crazy," I admitted, "but I'm sure."

I also wasn't doing this without a partial plan to avoid insolvency. The week before, I'd called up my old boss, Mr. Thomas, at the mortgage licensing firm. "I'd like to return," I told him, "but only if I can be there part-time." My plan was to work at the firm for half the day and spend the other half setting up a small furniture company. Can you believe the guy agreed? Around the office, he'd had a reputation as a bit of a bulldog, but if he believed in you, there was no one more loyal. I'll always appreciate that he gave me the chance to chase my dream.

Soon after, I came up with a name for my new venture: River Dog Furniture Co. I never did file the paperwork to form an LLC, but the company felt no less real to me. Soon I was building tables for two of my coworkers and one for my boss's middle son. And then after completing those projects, for two years, I didn't touch my tools.

I know that sounds nuts, and given how passionate I was upon returning from Georgia, it was. But I just let the rest of life get in the way of my dream. My part-time job eventually grew back into a full-time one, with more and more responsibilities and greater pay. I kept my tools, and week after week I promised myself that I'd get back into the garage. But then I somehow wouldn't. It's not that I'd lost the desire, much like I had never completely lost the desire to pursue a music career. But maybe making furniture was just meant to be my hobby, because I had no idea how to turn it into a business.

In the five years since Kelly and I had left Baylor and launched into our happily ever after, I'd held five different jobs, been fired once, cut our European mission short, and lost cherished family and friends. And now, with most of my twenties in the rearview mirror, I couldn't escape the thought that I should set aside my crazy furniture-building ideas and just grow up. In the midst of this confusion, Kelly and I decided it was time to take the next logical step—have kids.

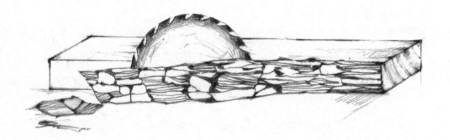

CHAPTER 7

Rough Cuts

Let's say I'm making a tabletop from eight-foot boards. There they are on the floor of the shop, lined up in nice rows and resembling what they will look like when they've been joined. Now I've got to prep them for that eventual union. It's incredibly important that this step be done well. Get it wrong, and it can create big problems down the road. In most shops, you use a face jointer and an edge planer to rake across the wood to square the boards and create a uniform thickness. It takes time to get each piece right. There will be waste and sawdust everywhere; parts of the board you may have loved will be gone forever. But when you're done, though the board is still a board, it's that much closer to fulfilling its ultimate purpose.

By the summer of 2006, Kelly was pregnant. Every day after work, we would go for long walks around the neighborhood, the whole time dreaming and talking about baby Harp. It was such an exciting time—until every evening when I once again noticed where we were actually living. Busy streets. Stray dogs. Overgrown lawns. The neighborhood was changing for the better, but slowly. Our fixer-upper was still as awesome as ever, but it was tiny and laid out in a way that would make it impossible to escape a wailing baby. Maybe it was time to cash in on our investment and move.

Here's the thing about parenting. Even before your child arrives, you begin looking at the world through a different lens. You want the best for that kid, even when he or she is still just a tiny dot on an ultrasound screen. As soon as I learned we were expecting, I began yearning for a house with a bigger backyard, in a neighborhood with a park close by, people walking their dogs—on leashes! A bohemian existence is great when you're a couple of newlyweds just trying to set up your life was my narrow-minded opinion. But now, with a child on the way, what I wanted had shifted. So we put our house up for sale and began looking for a more family-friendly home.

On April 30, 2007, we closed on the sale of our little white house. We'd purchased our fixer-upper for $120,000 less than two years before and were able to sell it for $165,000. The next day, we used the earnings from that sale to put a $20,000 down payment on our second home, this one in Richardson, a nice Dallas suburb. The closing went off without a hitch, and we moved into our new place on May 1. Nine days later, our son was born.

His arrival was a nail-biter for sure. We showed up at the hospital the night before Kelly would be induced. We spent the night watching reruns of *The Office* and tried to get some sleep. By six thirty the following morning, things were moving along fine. At seven, however, Kelly was being rushed into the OR for an emergency C-section because our baby's heart rate kept slowing. We were terrified. The medical team had wheeled her away so quickly that I'd barely had a chance to say good-bye. I stood alone with my delivery day mix CD in what we thought would be our delivery room and tried to pull myself together. The nurses eventually came and took me to the OR, and by seven thirty, I was cradling my son's little pink body. While the doctors sewed Kelly back up, I kept wondering, *Shouldn't somebody be taking care of this thing?* In that moment, I couldn't quite take it in that the "somebody" was me. Kelly was still coming in and out of consciousness because of all the anesthesia, and I was just trying to keep my head from spinning off my neck.

"What's his name?" asked the nurse as she lifted him from my arms so she could clean him up. Before then, we'd kept that an absolute secret. But now, to the first person who'd asked, I proudly replied, "Hudson Kenneth Harp." My grandfather, father, and I all had the middle name Kenneth. The tradition was alive. The nurse smiled approvingly. After she finished her duties and handed my son back to me, I felt like I should sign something or pay a cashier. It was weird. I went over to Kelly, who was just coming out of her drugged state, and held Hudson right up to her face. "He's beautiful," she whispered. She then closed her eyes and faded back to sleep.

During our couple of days in the hospital, we were advised to let the nurses take care of our baby overnight so we could get some rest. That went fine on the first evening, but on the second morning, Kelly woke me up, anxious that they hadn't yet brought him to her. I kept telling her everything was fine, but she was adamant. I should have believed her. The phone rang.

"Hi, Kelly," said a calm voice. "This is a nurse downstairs. Hudson has weakened and he's hypoglycemic. The doctor is almost here and we want to give him a feeding tube." I put Kelly in a wheelchair and we whipped through the halls. We got to the nursery in record time, and for the next three days, we stayed by our son's side. He had gone from a healthy seven pounds nine ounces at birth to a scrawny five pounds. He would rebound in the neonatal intensive care unit, but we remained terrified. The three of us—Kelly and I, as well as Kelly's mom, whom we call Mimi—took turns at Hud's side every hour he was in the NICU. Mimi insisted on taking the first shift so we could get some rest. Hours later, when Kelly went down to relieve her, she stood quietly at the door and listened to her mom saying to Hudson, "You've got to get big so you can go play at your new house, and so your mom can yell out the back door, 'Come on in, Hud, supper's ready!'" Kelly remembers that moment like it happened five minutes ago.

When our son was finally released from the hospital five days later, I wanted to take his nurse home with us. The entire earthly existence of this little miracle was now solely in our hands.

Those first few days back at home, I channeled all my worry into a project. It had been a couple of years since I'd built anything, and as a proud new father, I decided to build Hudson a big-boy bed and an armoire. Yeah, sure, our son was only days old, but I figured I'd get a jump on it. I was in the garage late one Friday evening when Kelly's cell rang.

"This is the lab at the hospital," said a nurse. "We did some screenings on your son while he was here, and he has a condition called MCAD. Please make sure you feed him every three hours without exception, and call the doctor first thing on Monday."

"I'm sorry, um . . . who is this?" stammered Kelly. "And MCAD—what?"

The nurse explained that MCAD—or medium-chain acyl-CoA dehydrogenase deficiency—is a metabolic disorder that prevents the body from breaking down certain fats and turning them into energy. It's a genetic enzyme deficiency, and apparently Kelly and I, both silent carriers of the recessive gene, had passed it on to our beloved Hudson. That's why he'd become hypoglycemic in the hospital. It's also why we had to be sure he ate regularly to keep his blood sugar from dropping to a dangerous low.

If we'd been riddled with anxiety at our son's birth, we were petrified now. The one piece of good news, our doctor later told us, was that the condition could eventually get progressively easier to manage the older he got. In Hudson's case, it has. In fact, you'd never even know it's there.

But on the evening when we got the message from the lab, we went into survival mode, starting six months of feeding our son around the clock every three hours as we'd been instructed. My wife stayed up for the eleven p.m. feeding and I took the two a.m. shift. I remember sitting on the couch with Hudson, watching reruns of *Family Ties* as I tried to feed him and put him down, knowing that a short few hours later, I'd be back up and getting ready for my workday. Both Kelly and I were beyond exhausted.

Later I realized that I never did get to press play on my delivery day CD. It's funny how life can sometimes just sweep you along. One minute, you're creating CDs and making plans, and the next, you're scrambling to keep your child alive. In carpentry, there's a rule: measure twice, cut once. Yet no matter how accurate you've been in your measurements, chances are, you're going to make a mistake, or something will be slightly off and you're going to have to adjust. But hang in there—don't lose hope. Keep making your way through the rough cuts—and, yeah, you'll finally figure it out.

* * *

Kelly and I had decided that once Hudson was born, she'd trade in her teaching job to work at home as a full-time mom. She still dreamed of possibly becoming a college professor one day, but she first wanted to focus on nurturing our son. Hudson's metabolic disorder had suddenly made that more necessary than ever. It also meant that it was time for me to get a big-boy job so I could better provide for my family.

My position at the mortgage licensing firm was going well and I enjoyed my coworkers, but I had no benefits. My hourly rate was excellent, but I'd never intended for it to be my forever job, so I began searching. I searched my heart, my head, and the internet. For a hot minute, I thought about med school. The nurses and doctors who'd guided us through Hudson's crisis had helped us greatly, and I wanted to do the same for others. But who was I kidding? School had never been my thing. I switched gears and began looking for something more administrative, a job similar to my current one, only in the medical field. I flipped through the contact list in my head and made some calls.

Back at Baylor, Kelly had a sorority sister Jeffie. I'd once fixed her car—a skill I'd picked up during a childhood full of repairing crappy cars—and she was eternally grateful. Kelly had heard that Jeffie's husband, Chris, was working at a medical company in Dallas. She suggested I ring him.

"Chris, hi, this is Clint Harp." Years earlier they had supported us on our Paris journey, so this was a bit of a reconnection.

"Yes, Clint!" he said. "How are ya, bud?"

"Well, I'm great," I said, "just looking for a job. I thought I'd see what you had going on over there. Right now, I'm the director of operations for a mortgage licensing firm and would love to do something like that in the medical field."

Chris thought for a moment. "I'll tell you what," he said. "We really don't have any openings like that here. But there is a position open for a sales rep in our Houston office." Before I could inquire about the details, he added, "By the end of the first year, you should be making six figures."

While I was all in on the salary—we really needed the money—I wasn't sold on the sales field. For crying out loud, during my stint as a copier salesman, I could remember lying in bed at night feeling my heart pound from the stress of needing to meet sales quotas. Medical sales especially made me uncomfortable, although at the time I couldn't tell why. And this might sound strange if you've never lived in Texas, but even though I enjoyed our time in the big city of Dallas, I never saw myself moving to the Houston metropolis. For one thing, I was raised an Atlanta Braves fan and couldn't stand the Houston Astros. For another, a large city with millions of people and horrific traffic sounded awful to me back then. But all that went to hell when I heard the words *six figures*. Over one hundred thousand dollars in one year? Go 'stros!

Four months after that call, we'd sold our house—yes, the one we'd just purchased—and loaded up our U-Haul. I'd landed the job and we were going to Houston. I strapped four-month-old Hudson into his car seat and we made our way down Interstate 45. A moving truck filled with everything we owned trailed behind. On the way, electronic road signs flashed warnings at us: "Houston is experiencing inclement weather. Tropical storms and hurricanes are on the way. TURN AROUND." We ignored the signs and kept right on driving. Six figures! 401(k)! Paid vacation! Move it or lose it, hurricane, we're coming through!

*   *   *

Sales is a wonderful career for those that are passionate about it. I've had the pleasure of working with amazing salespeople in my life and had great experiences with people who love the field. But if you don't love it, it can be a nightmare, just like anything else you're doing but don't really want to do. And when it came down to it, I hated selling infusion therapy for all the same reasons I'd once deplored making cold calls for copy machines. In this case, my potential customers were hospital social workers and case managers and of course doctors. Here I was, this preppy thirty-year-old goofball in a suit, trying to sell a medical pump as I attempted to bridge gaps in culture, knowledge (as in I had none), gender, and just about every other chasm you can imagine. Bridging gaps is something I'm all about, but it didn't feel right for me while also trying to make a sale. I'm sure if I'd truly gotten to know those I was attempting to connect with, they'd have as much in common with me as the next person. But when you show up at a hospital, peddling pumps, you have only seconds to establish a good rapport. I did it by sweetening the deal. "Would y'all like some brownies?" I'd typically start with. *So creative.* Most would show moderate interest and welcome me into their office. Flattery and my dimples—in place of much knowledge of medicine—got me in. And when Christmas rolled around, I was slinging around Godiva chocolates to anyone within range. That worked okay at first, but then it started to feel gross.

But I stuck with my golden handcuffs. I kept my head down for the first two years and tried to just suppress my complaints. For one thing, I wanted to do right by the friend who'd given me the opportunity. For another, Hudson was growing up fast, and we were talking about having a second child. Not only was I earning enough to support the family, but both of the cars we now owned had been purchased without a financial struggle, and I was comfortably making my monthly student loan payments. On most days, I was home before five p.m. Talk about an ideal situation. And yet it just didn't feel right.

Around that time, Kelly was working with a life coach, Paul, who was really helping her think about next steps. We knew him from church. Paul was probably in his early fifties then, a friendly guy with an easy smile and a kind demeanor. Earlier in life, he'd found his way up the corporate ladder, and while he'd been financially successful, he was one of those guys who'd moved at a thousand miles an hour and had very little margin in his life for anything other than work. Because of this, he lost a lot of the things that meant the most to him. As he worked to rebuild his life, he no longer wanted to make enormous amounts of money or become known in his industry. Rather, he wanted nothing more than to just walk with other people through their pain and struggle, the kind of heartache he'd lived through.

Kelly knew how miserable I was and suggested I talk with Paul, but I just didn't feel comfortable with the idea. Like a lot of men, I'd always been more closed off to talking openly about my issues and emotions.

One afternoon, I pulled onto our street just as Paul was leaving our house after meeting with Kelly. He drove up beside me in the middle of the road. It was raining outside, but we rolled down our windows anyway.

"I know you don't know me very well," he said, "but I know you. I've been where you've been and I know what you're going through. I'm here to tell you it's okay, and I'd love to spend some time talking with you, if you want."

I'll admit that I teared up a bit while Paul was talking. He absolutely saw inside my heart at the moment. But as he drove away, I thought, *No way. I don't need a shrink.*

A few months later, though, I knew I needed to have someone besides Kelly to confide in. I gave him a call, and we met at a Starbucks in uptown Houston. Our conversation flowed easily, like two friends just trading stories. We ended that meeting by making plans for the next one.

I began meeting with Paul every other week at the coffee shop. As I grew more comfortable, I'd dig in and share more of my life and hopes for the future, and I'd find myself crying my eyes out in public as I went deeper. I told Paul about the places where I felt stuck and the dreams I'd once had to build furniture. We talked a lot about happiness, and what it meant to actually *be* happy. "True happiness is about being the most honest and true form of yourself," Paul would tell me. "You can't be happy if you're living a lie." And by "lie," he didn't necessarily mean stepping out on your wife or having a secret family stashed away in Nevada. The kind of lie he was talking about wasn't so obvious or extreme. It could be waking up every morning, doing a job you never wanted to do in a city you never wanted to live in, all for the sake of the dollars.

Hello.

Over the next two years, Paul would have me read books (*Man's Search for Meaning* by Viktor Frankl was on his must-read list); watch many movies (he had me dust off *Field of Dreams*, starring Kevin Costner, whose character was crazy enough to build a baseball field in his backyard so that famous players of the past would come back from the dead and play there); walk silently and think; walk silently and *not* think; dream with Kelly; and be brutally honest about my fears. It was intense. When we'd meet, he'd often ask me one question in particular: "What do you really want to do, Clint?" And the answer that kept bubbling up inside me from a deep place was this: go build furniture. Paul was careful never to tell me what to do; that was my choice. "You're the main character in your own story," he'd remind me. "Everybody else is your supporting cast, just as you play a supporting role in others' stories. As the lead, you've gotta decide how you want your narrative to unfold."

During this time, I stayed in my job, and in February 2010, Kelly and I welcomed our daughter Holland, named after the country where we'd made such fond memories. Also at this time and with the blessing of my boss, and a small but resurfacing desire to ease back into ministry, I even took on a second job. During our last few months in Dallas and upon relocating to Houston, we'd returned to church, our first time back in the pews since our days in Europe. When the need arose for a pastor at the small church plant we attended up in The Woodlands, about thirty miles north of our home, I was asked to consider the job. Never mind that I was still sorting out my beliefs. And never mind that I had no formal training as a head pastor. I agreed to take the position on a part-time basis. The job lasted only a year before the church planting effort was disbanded, but my own faith in real community where people could search for God and love and iron out their issues was bolstered by the experience. And we gained real and close friend-ships that have lasted to this day.

What's crazy is that I'd never wanted to be a pastor or a salesman. I'm thankful for the many pastors who've had such an impact on me, and Lord knows we need good, honest salespeople in the ranks. I respect them. I just didn't want to *be* them. When I'd show up for my appointments with Paul, he'd occasionally introduce me to the person he'd been meeting with before our appointment. "This is Clint," he'd joke. "He's in medical sales and he's a pastor. And you know what? He doesn't want to do either!"

I might not have liked my sales job, but I was pretty dang good at it. By year three, I'd traded the suit and tie for scrubs, which is what a lot of my target clients wore. It was a way for me to fit in. In the movie *Patch Adams*, there's a scene where a young Dr. Adams, played by Robin Williams, disrupts the hospital establishment by grabbing a red ball syringe, placing it on his nose, and creating spontaneous entertainment for sick children in the ward. The kids loved it. I loved it, too. That was my inspiration to put on my light blue scrubs and navy Chuck Taylors and show up at the hospital as a new man. I wasn't there to sell anything anymore. I was there to connect and build trust, and that's what I did. I found that taking just a few minutes to connect with real patients, and not just the caseworkers and doctors, alleviated some of the stress of my job.

But the more patients I met, the more it started to bother me that I'd sometimes see dollar signs hanging over their heads. Their prolonged illnesses usually meant greater profit; the more severe their conditions, the more money I earned. Some people can do that kind of work with no misgivings and an honest ability to separate the patient from the profit (my company happened to be full of them), and we need those people in our world. But I had a very hard time with it, and I often shared those reservations with Kelly. Day by day, one sales call at a time, it felt like a little piece of me was dying.

*   *   *

In summer 2010, our annual sales meeting rolled around. My manager, Chris, stood at the front of the conference room and introduced a bunch of new faces. "This team is going to work with us to take our business up to the next level," he announced. They'd been brought in to further train us, to turn us into the kind of salespeople who would exponentially increase the company's revenue. Outwardly, I pasted on a smile. Inwardly, I was stressing out.

I don't usually get too nervous, but I was nervous on this day. By then I'd already told Chris, who was also a dear friend, that I often thought about eventually quitting this job to go for my dream of building furniture. I knew that in bringing in these sales trainers, he was just doing his job to build the company. But for me, things were more complicated: I'd either have to sell myself out by entering a six-month commitment to work with this new team, or cleverly find another exit.

We were split up into groups and each group was assigned a sales mentor. Mine was Steve, the main guy. As he approached our group, I was literally sweating. *Sell out? Buy in? Escape? Call a bluff? Fake illness? Crap, he's standing right in front of me introducing himself and offering his hand.*

Steve took a seat across from me. "Clint, what do you want out of this training?" he asked. "How can I help you?"

"So the thing is," I began, with my throat tight, "I actually don't want to do this. I don't know when, but I'm quitting soon. I want to build furniture. It's crazy, I know, but it's what I want to do. I'm sorry. I don't want to waste your time, and honestly, I don't know what to do, but . . . yeah . . . there you go."

"Well, Clint," he said, "that's amazing. I love it."

Did he just say what I think he said? Yep. "Years ago," he continued, "I quit my job, jumped in an RV, and traveled around the country reconnecting with family and friends. It was one of the greatest adventures of my life. It's part of what led me to this job, which I love. I'm sure you're going to be just fine, and I'm excited to walk with you on this part of your journey."

I wish I had a picture of my face in the moment. I was dumbfounded. I felt like I'd just been visited by a fairy godfather. I half expected to later tell my coworkers about my meeting with Steve, only to have them look at me confused and say, "Steve? There's no Steve here, Clint." But he was there. He was real. And he was saying exactly what I needed to hear.

Steve and I stayed in touch. Every week over the next six months, he'd check in with me by phone. Sometimes we'd have a conference call with a few of my coworkers who were also working with Steve, and after it ended, he'd call me directly, just to see how I was doing. It's amazing that Chris let me stay on board even after he knew I was planning to move on. That's grace. That's also friendship.

Our team training, we were told, would culminate in a final presentation by each sales rep. We were supposed to discuss our plans for success in the coming year and include graphs, sales figures, and projections. *Yeah, right.* The morning of my presentation was just before Thanksgiving, and I had something else in mind.

I was surer than I'd ever been that I was going to pursue my dream. So I didn't mess around. Instead, I got up and talked about the patients I loved and the connections I'd made. I passionately shared stories of the lives I'd seen changed by the company's products. In the front row was the president of the company, Rick, and I promise you I saw him shed a tear. Months afterward, Chris would tell me that Rick later said in his thick Texas accent, "Yeah, I knew Clint was gone after that presentation." He was right. It was my farewell speech.

*   *   *

By spring 2011—and nearly two years into my meetings with life coach Paul—I came home from work one day and plopped down in a corner of our living room. Little Hudson was playing with his toys in the middle of the floor while Kelly was feeding Holland. She knew by the look on my face and the tears in my eyes that I was dealing with something serious. She put down our daughter and came and sat beside me on the couch.

"What's up, babe?" she asked.

"This is it, Kelly," I murmured.

"What do you mean?"

"I mean I can't do this job anymore," I told her. "I can't. I know we don't have as much money saved up as we want for us to build a furniture business, but I cannot continue this way. The feeling is so strong that I can't ignore it anymore."

"Okay, Clint," she said. "I'm with you. We can do this." Her support was powerful.

The rest of my family was also behind me. My mom and stepdad, because of the wild life of constant moving they'd led, learning to make it through the toughest of situations, were cheering me on in full force. The same was true of my stepmom, who surprised me with her readiness to almost push me over the risky cliff herself! My dad, though encouraging, was a bit more cautious. He wanted me to be sure I was ready to walk away from a six-figure salary with benefits. I actually loved that he was concerned. Having grown up spending only every other weekend living with him, I was touched by his hovering over me with genuine fatherly concern. It made me feel like I did during the days when we would wrestle on the ground and he would rub his scratchy chin on my face and on my bare chest. I loved those moments, and loved feeling like he was trying to hold me tight. I needed that. I needed all of it.

I also knew it was time to take the leap. The next day at work, I called Chris and gave him my two weeks' notice. Two more weeks of a secure paycheck, and that would be it. Two more weeks of structured workdays. Two more weeks before I stepped into the wild unknown.

I hung up with Chris and sent off a text to Kelly and Paul. It was a picture of a guy jumping off a cliff, arms spread out wide, in a free fall.

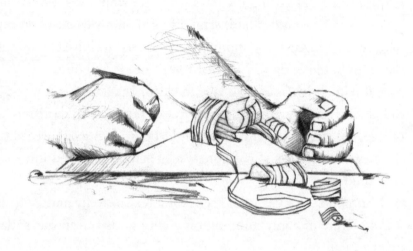

CHAPTER 8

Handcrafted

I never get tired of crafting every single component of a table: the top, the supports, the skirt, the legs. In the early days, when I chose to use reclaimed wood, I'd have to be inventive. Over time I found that making a leg out of scraps was so much more satisfying than buying premanufactured stock. When I'm joining boards to create a leg, I begin with finding the right amount of wood. Let's say I've got six boards, each measuring approximately 1 x 4 x 72 inches. A table leg is roughly 29 inches long and 3 x 3 inches thick. If I cut my boards in half and then stack five of them on top of one another, I end up with a stack measuring roughly 3.5 x 3 x 36 inches. I then glue those up and leave them to dry overnight between some big sturdy clamps (I like to use "cabinet clamps"). I don't hold back on the glue, but I also wipe off the excess that escapes when the clamps are tightened. By morning, they're ready to go. Once they're dry, a quick couple of passes over the jointer and through the planer gives me a nice square stock with which to make my legs.

"Clint, check these out," Kelly said. "I found some pics online where people took pallets and made furniture from them. Thought you might like that."

And that's how I got the idea to build with reclaimed wood. Kelly had actually shown me the photographs before I quit my job, when we both knew it was inevitable. Over the next few months, as I worked up the courage to go for my dream, the pictures served as my inspiration. They got me thinking about how much I wanted to build furniture.

But in what style? By the time I traded my scrubs and shiny name tag for a tool belt, Kelly and I had developed some strong ideas. For one, we wanted to create the kind of original pieces that could look as good in a SoHo loft as they could in a sprawling Texas ranch house. I was fairly sure our design ideas would be costly, so I'd already called up a lumberyard to price things out. I wanted to know approximately how much it would set us back to build a single table.

A guy with a heavy Texas drawl had answered the phone: "Mernin', Dawsen Lummeryard, whadyaneed?"

"Um, yes," I said, "Is this Dawson's Lumberyard?" (For the record, this wasn't the real name, but otherwise the conversation went down exactly like this, meaning I could only understand every fourth word. The lumber world, I'd soon learn, has a type of slang and banter all its own.)

"Yeah," he answered. "So whadyaneed?"

"I need some wood for a table."

"Right. Three quar', four quar', or six quar'?"

"Excuse me?" I said. "What's a 'quar'?"

"You ever ordered lummer before, son?"

"Um, no, not really."

"I'm askin' how thick you want your lummer. Four quar' is 'bout an inch. Six quar' is like an inchanahalf."

"Oh. Right. Of course," I said. "I guess I'll go with four 'quar,' then. Let's see how much that'll cost."

"You got a planer and a jointer?" he asked. I told him no.

"Well, you'll need 'em if it's rough cut." Rough cut, he explained, was usually the cheapest wood because it hadn't been prepared in any way for further use.

One call, and it had been confirmed: when it came to lumber, I was a complete idiot. In my previous job as a medical salesman, there'd been plenty of times when I'd had zero clue what I was talking about, so I did my best to fake it till I made it. I thought the same would be true for lumber. I mean, liver disease is one thing, but wood? I was pretty sure I could figure that out.

I did know a little something about the different varieties of wood, thanks to my granddad. From him, I'd learned that old growth pine is usually darker and richer and displays the evidence of a slower growth cycle and older age with its tighter grain. New pine is grown quickly and aggressively, so the distance between the grain is much wider than in wood that has grown slowly and consistently over a longer period of time. My grandfather used to show me the end of a log and point out the tight grain, which occasionally would be interrupted by a massive gap before the next growth ring. "What do you think happened that year?" he'd ask.

But that was about the extent of my wood and lumber knowledge. And now I saw that not only was I on a steep learning curve, but this whole thing was going to be expensive. When I finally explained my full order to the lumber salesman, he estimated I'd need about a hundred dollars' worth of rough-cut wood to build a decent table. That didn't sound too bad, until I started doing the math. If I wanted to put together, say, twenty tables, that'd run me a minimum of a couple thousand bucks. Bottom line: We couldn't afford it. That's when I started thinking about those pictures Kelly had shown me. When I saw the pallet furniture, made from reclaimed wood, something in me was unlocked.

"There are pallets everywhere," I told Kelly. "And you know what? They're free!" I figured it couldn't be that hard to pull a few apart and make a table. Yes, pallets are short. And sure, they don't typically have wood thick enough for legs. But I'd cross that bridge when I got to it.

Around that time, I caught a documentary called *A Man Named Pearl*, which chronicled the inspiring story of a self-taught topiary artist in Bishopville, South Carolina. Born to a sharecropper, Pearl Fryar grew up in Clinton, North Carolina, before moving to Bishopville, where he worked at a canning factory. Later, when he bought a house for his family in a predominantly white area, Pearl was spurned by neighbors who didn't think an African American man would properly take care of his yard. Rather than battling their disdain with anger he decided he'd win yard of the month. He started rescuing plants from the waste bin of a local nursery and the magic began. Pearl carefully grew and tended his plants and turned them into beautiful topiaries.

As I pursued my own dream of building furniture from reclaimed wood, I could not stop thinking about this artist, who took the seeds of hate and a pile of discarded plants and used them to create a garden. In fact, I talked about Pearl so much that my mentor, Paul, suggested I call him. That seemed outlandish to me.

"Uh, right, Paul," I said, chuckling. "I don't even know this guy, and I'm just supposed to dial him up? Any idea how I'd even get his number?"

"Nope," he said, "but I'm sure you'll find it. Call him."

This conversation happened five or six times before I decided I'd try. *This is so stupid*, I thought as I picked up the phone. First I called the Bishopville Chamber of Commerce. The woman who answered didn't have Pearl's number, but she knew a local professor who was Pearl's friend, and she gave me his number instead. Minutes later, I was on the line with this friend. "What a story you have there," he said after I'd recounted the personal journey that had led me in search of Pearl. I was shocked when he then gave me Pearl's number.

I called right away. His wife, Mrs. Fryar, answered and told me her husband was in the garden. She welcomed me to call back later. I thanked her profusely and rang their home every day over the next four days until I reached the man himself.

"Hello?" answered a baritone voice I recognized from the documentary.

"Hi, I'm Clint!" I said excitedly. "Wow, it's great to finally talk to you, Mr. Fryar."

"Thank you," he said. "You can call me Pearl."

We talked for around fifteen minutes. I told him how inspired I was by his story, and shared a little of my own. As the conversation progressed, that magical moment I'd rehearsed in my head beforehand, when I'd hear something so extraordinary that it would totally rock my world and alter my perspective, never happened. But it didn't have to, because his story already had. His life was this beautiful tapestry that spoke volumes. And almost as soon as I put down the phone from that call, I understood what Paul had known all along: it was never about finding Pearl. It was about being willing to set out on a journey that might seem ridiculous, to chase something that appeared unreachable. It was also about talking to someone who'd already done what I'd once been afraid to do—go out on a limb. Doing so had meant overcoming the seed of doubt that is hardwired into us. Reaching out to Pearl was, for me, a reminder of what can happen when we trade the reasonable and predictable for what is daringly possible.

*　*　*

Around the same time I quit my job, my sweet younger sister, Suzanne, was making her own leap and getting married. She'd been brave enough to venture from her sleepy hometown in North

Georgia to New York City, where she had met someone and fallen in love. I was as happy for her as I was proud. And we wouldn't have missed the wedding for the world. But as I boarded a plane to New York with Kelly and our two kids, I was thinking that it had been pretty dumb for me to quit my job *before* a pricey trip. Couldn't I have waited a few more weeks? At the time, I hadn't thought so. It was then or never.

That trip to New York was life-changing. After celebrating my sister's nuptials, we stayed on a few days to explore the city. Kelly and I felt like we'd been transported back to Paris, only with kids this time. New York has its own pace and heartbeat, one that thumps loud and strong. We wanted to walk everywhere, try all different kinds of foods, take in the sights, the sounds, the creativity and artistry around every corner, feel the electricity and fervor. We journeyed to Brooklyn, with its green Prospect Park, and fell in love. Back in Manhattan's Flatiron District, we wandered into ABC Carpet & Home, a massive six-story home goods shop. The place was filled with level after level of beautiful designs, many of them handmade by and sourced from local artisans. Kelly struck up a conversation with a store employee who happened to be involved in purchasing. My wife, she's something. Her belief in me has always been more than I could ask for. I'd not yet built a single table for our little company, and she was already selling our creations! We told the woman about our company, and she gave us a card. We kept that card for years. Though we never reached out (mostly because of my own insecurity), that connection, as well as the whole experience in New York, gave us hope for where we might end up. We were both so renewed and inspired by the experience.

"You know what," I daydreamed aloud to Kelly, "we could move here." It was true: now that I was no longer tethered to a day job, we could relocate anywhere in the world. Around the time I'd quit, we'd put our house on the market, so we weren't tied down to Houston. Everything felt wide-open to us, and New York City represented the countless possibilities. We left there feeling energized.

We carried that motivation home with us, excitedly planning the next stage of our journey. Kelly and I didn't want to simply make and sell beautiful things. We wanted each piece to tell a story, to have a meaning beyond its basic function. We wanted to build furniture that would bring people together, that would make them laugh and reflect and celebrate. We wanted them to feel the love and warmth and intention behind each of our creations. And by the way, it helped that I wasn't the first entrepreneur in the family—Kelly was. A couple of years earlier, she'd begun sewing children's clothes, as well as creating designs on towels and blankets. She set up a small business, Alacrity Designs, and had accounts in Austin, Houston, Dallas, and even one in New York City. Though she eventually folded the venture so she could focus on creating home goods for our new company, the experience had taught her plenty, and she brought those lessons to our conversations about how we should move forward.

As soon as our bags were unpacked from the New York trip, we sat down at our kitchen table and began mapping out what our business might look like. Yes, I'd build tables, but what else would we make, and how would Kelly and I split up the responsibilities of owning a small business? What materials would we use? Would we hire employees, and if so, how would we treat them? What were our values as co-owners of a brand-new enterprise? We also discussed cobbling together a website and imagined how, with absolutely no experience, we'd sell enough of our creations to earn a living. Was it a bit insane? Absolutely. But for a couple of wide-eyed idealists, it actually sounded plausible.

And, oh yeah, what would we call this whole thing? The original name I'd come up with but never registered, River Dog Furniture Co., was inspired by all the dogs my grandparents had running around the Roost back home on the Chattahoochee River. But Kelly wasn't feeling it. She liked the name, but she didn't think it fit with how our startup was evolving: we'd settled on a business plan in which I would craft furniture and Kelly would curate and sell home goods. She was convinced that our family's name should somehow be included in the company's name, and that it should leave us room to grow beyond furniture and home goods. She was right. That's when it hit us: Harp Design Co. Done. It felt perfect. Now we needed a logo.

Kelly sketched out some ideas. In the end, she used a free design program on the internet to create the final graphic, a simple but impactful rendering of our company's name inside a square. We still proudly display that logo as a representation of our business and a reminder of our early days of dreaming. Every time I see it, whether on a T-shirt in my drawer, stamped on a cutting board, or on social media, I enjoy knowing that it came from the mind of my wife, who quietly sat at the table with no safety net beneath her and framed it up.

*   *   *

When the first morning rolled around where I would jump in the shop and build some tables, I grabbed my keys and drove off in search of pallets. I landed at our local H-E-B grocery store. "Do you have any old wood pallets you're getting rid of here?" I asked the store manager. He did, and he said I was more than welcome to head to the store's back entrance and dig through the dumpster in search of them. Unplanned by either of us, Kelly happened to show up at that same grocery store that morning. And for whatever reason, she drove into the parking lot through the back entrance. There I was, standing by the dumpster in ratty jeans and a T-shirt, holding a filthy pallet, when a black SUV rolled up next to me. From the back seat, Hudson and Holland stared at me with their jaws hanging open, as if to say, "Daddy, have you lost your mind?"

In a way, I had. The old me, the one who had grown comfortable with a six-figure status quo, was disappearing. Old priorities, deep-seated beliefs, and preconceived notions of what my life should look like—all were fading away. In their place was a rough, raw, and humbling hunt for the materials I needed to craft our future.

Kelly and the kids drove away, and I got back to dumpster diving. Those first pallets were pretty gnarly. But I didn't care. I just took whatever didn't look like it was going to make me sick. I drove a Honda Pilot at the time, and I could fit four or five pallets in the car if I didn't close the back hatch. I'd go back and forth from my house to a store, loading the car, heading home, dropping everything off, then repeating the whole routine. In those days, I mostly found pallets that were four feet by four feet with planks just under three-quarters of an inch thick. I later discovered that pallets measuring twelve feet and longer existed. Some were even made from hardwood. But in those early days, it was me and a bunch of short pine pallets.

Surprise, surprise: It was a lot tougher than I'd thought it would be to pry those things apart. A few of them would just pop loose, but most were as tough as the nails holding them together. It would take me a day just to tear six to eight pallets apart. A whole day! But after about a week, I had a nice stack of planks. I was creating my own lumber supply and getting one step closer to making a piece of furniture about which someone might say, "Wait, you built *that* from a pallet?"

One of the greatest influences in my transformation, both personal and entrepreneurial, has been my wife. Kelly knows me better than anyone on the planet. She has pinpointed things about me that I still can't muster the courage to admit to myself. With clairvoyant skill, she has lovingly pegged me many times. And yet, for the first few months of our insane journey, I tried my hardest to convince her that everything was fine. I was confident I could positively spin the fact that by the end of the summer, for all my dumpster diving and pallet pulling, I hadn't actually produced anything. I had no tables. No income. No prospects. No anything. Just a pile of planks on the garage floor and a few half-baked ideas in my notebook. "Don't worry, honey," I'd say to convince her. "It's all coming together." She wasn't buying it.

We began clashing. All the time. There were so many arguments, they made our former "Butter Offensive" seem like the good ol' days. It was intense: yelling, crying, awkward silences. We weren't just in over our heads—we were at the bottom of the ocean.

One weekend, Kelly went to visit a friend in her hometown of Tyler. She took the kids with her.

"When you get back," I boldly proclaimed, "I'm going to have some tables to show you."

"Really, Clint?" she said, smiling, one eyebrow raised.

"You bet, babe," I assured her. "You'll see."

Kelly challenged me to see how many tables I could finish during her three days away. I was determined to show my wife just how excited she should be about how bright our future was. I kissed her and the kids good-bye and got to work.

Day one. After hitting it hard for ten hours straight, I went out to buy some groceries. I pulled up and noticed a construction site in a nearby lot. I went over to investigate, and that's when I spotted it: a massive woodpile headed for the landfill. *Jackpot.* I drove right up to the enormous garbage pile of 2x4s, 2x6s, and even 3x3s and 4x4s. *I can make legs with this stuff!* I thought. I was scrambling to fill our SUV when I discovered a deep little pocket of gold: lying before me were dozens of scaffolding planks made of a dense oak that had just been tossed in the trash!

Up to then, I'd been finding and reclaiming pallets (almost always pine) and fence slats (almost always cedar). But every once in a while I would notice a little something different in a pallet and take a little closer look. The occasional walnut board was easy to identify, and oak was, too. Specifically, red oak was really common, but it was finding the rarer white oak that could really make my day. At the construction site that day with those scaffolding planks, I uncovered a whole heap of white oak, some of the richest I'd seen. A few of the boards were as long as four feet, and all were two and a quarter inches thick. By the time I'd finished loading the back of our SUV, it was sagging a bit.

Construction sites! I kept thinking, speeding off as if I were driving a getaway car. *Why didn't I think of this before!?* This was a whole new world. Sure, I'd be able to find pallets, but real lumber? That was a revelation.

Day two. By this time, I was working with all the tools my grandfather had bought me, and I'd also started adding some others to my collection, like a planer. I'd purchased the most affordable one I could find and used it to create a uniform thickness with the pallet wood. I'd designed a tabletop that looked something like a section of wood floor. There'd be twelve rows of planks, with three boards in each row. Those three boards would be either 18, 24, or 30 inches long and would alternate by row so they'd always overlap, just like a hardwood floor. With this approach, I could use pallets to make six-foot-long tabletops. My goal was to come up with a system that would allow me to quickly produce three of those tabletops in one day, which would leave me plenty of time to craft and attach the table skirts and legs.

It was a good plan, but I got distracted. When I walked into our garage on that second day and saw all that amazing oak scaffolding I'd collected, I could not resist. I picked up a piece and shoved it in the planer. It was a tool I couldn't afford to replace, and yet I came dangerously close to burning out the motor as I ran that dense white oak through it. But oh, how glorious it looked! Just like with the pallet wood, it would start out looking dirty and mangled, but after I ran it through the machine, it would be gloriously transformed. I was hooked.

I decided that in addition to the three tabletops from pallet wood, I'd also make a workbench from this thick and hefty oak. I'd build it in the same fashion as the pallet tables, with the tops looking like a wood floor. Away I went. I laid out the pieces for what would eventually become the top of the workbench. I set up the dado blade on the table saw and cut out tongue-and-groove joints on each board. I dry-fit everything and made sure it all worked together perfectly. The next morning, or day three, I glued up and clamped three tops—the workbench top and two tabletops—and started work on the bases.

Later that afternoon, Kelly pulled up in front of our house. Spread out on the garage floor were my three tops, still in clamps and covered in hardened glue. On the other side of the garage sat the beginnings of a few legs and skirts. No finished tables.

"Hey, babe, welcome home," I said as she got out of the car. I met her out front so she couldn't catch a glimpse of what was—and wasn't—inside my makeshift shop. "Missed you guys!"

"Aww, missed you, too!" she said. I hugged her and the kids. "Let's take our stuff inside and get the kids settled, and then I want to see tables!" she exclaimed.

"Um, yeah," I said. "Let's do that."

When Kelly came back from Tyler and found not a single completed table, it lit a time bomb between us. I had not fulfilled my promise. Nor had I done something else I'd told her I'd do: take notes while building so we could get an idea of how we might make the business profitable. I had no excuse. I'd simply lost focus, as I sometimes do. I got excited about a new idea and allowed myself to be sidetracked at a time when I needed to concentrate. I was definitely taking the whole venture very seriously, but I was handling it all my way, and my way wasn't cutting it.

The arguing intensified. We were getting good at lashing out from the depths of our own personal fears and frustrations. An uneasy feeling hung over our house and affected everything and everyone inside it. Hudson and Holland, then four and one years old, respectively, could sense it. I'm sure even Maddie, our little beagle, who'd always been so emotionally connected to Kelly and me, could feel it, too. The excitement of setting off on this great adventure had evaporated, and in its place was a familiar feeling of failure that I carried around with me constantly. I knew I had to do something to get us back on track.

During my work on the tables over the weekend I had started thinking about how similar the garage was to a sweat lodge. In some Native American cultures, I'd heard, sweat lodges were fairly common. The incredibly basic Clint understanding of the idea was that you sit inside a steamy room and sweat out your impurities in order to essentially hit the emotional or spiritual reset button. Something I was in need of. We humans often find ourselves haunted by past failures, threatened by our insecurities, and terrified that our inadequacies will catch up with us and reveal us to be phonies. Or at least I do. If these emotions build up and fester, they can destroy us from the inside out.

Though I initially contemplated pitching a tent, I, the do-it-yourself guy, decided I'd make my own sweat lodge. What could be hotter than a garage in Houston? (Don't try this at home!)

Temperatures had consistently climbed north of 100 degrees every day that summer. So on Monday morning, I went into the garage, closed the door, and got to work. I'm not really sure what I did that day. I know I didn't build anything. I think I mostly tore apart pallets. And thought. And sweated. A lot. By day's end, I'd probably dropped ten pounds in perspiration alone.

I dragged myself into the house that evening, took a shower, and sat down on the couch with Kelly. This was it. This was the moment. I'd sweated, hammered, sawed, and prayed out all my crap. I was finally ready to face myself and my wife.

"Kelly, I'm an idiot," I told her. "I'm scared, and I honestly have no idea what I'm doing. And I'm sorry."

"Okay," she said. "I can work with this. We're good."

What? What did she just say? This wasn't how I'd seen the conversation going. I'm sure my confusion showed on my face, so Kelly clarified.

"Clint, you quit a job in sales to go for a dream, and yet you've been selling me all summer long," she said. "I know you. You can't sell me. And when you try to sell me, it makes me scared, because I know you're hiding something. Don't sell me, please. Just tell me what's going on and we'll be good."

And then we actually *were* good.

In the following weeks, Kelly and I would go on walks around our neighborhood just about every afternoon. It was still terribly hot, but we went anyway. We'd just walk. Talk. Dream. And just be together, with our kids riding along in the double stroller. Yes, sometimes we still argued, but the disagreements took a different tenor. We weren't tearing each other apart. We were pushing each other to grow. We were asking each other the hard questions and actually listening to each other's responses. Best of all, I was no longer hiding from Kelly. Not that I'd been successful at bluffing her in the first place.

Every day on our strolls, we'd walk by a man, easily in his late seventies, who was painting his whole house, section by section, one afternoon at a time, beneath the scorching sun. First, he sanded it down before even thinking about the first drop of paint. Weeks would go by and his ladder wouldn't move an inch while he concentrated on one specific area. He was determined. He was patient. He was also smart, waiting until the shade rested on his specific work area. And he was meticulous. Slow and steady. By the end of that summer, his house was done, and it was gorgeous. Kelly and I saw in that man's efforts what it would to take for us to be successful. We'd have to commit to our venture for the long haul. It wasn't going to be easy, but if we stuck with it, it would be beautiful.

It was on one of our last walks that summer that Kelly said to me, "I'd like to go back and get my master's." She'd held on to her desire to teach at the collegiate level, and through her sessions with Paul, she'd come back around to the idea of pursuing something that was just for her. When we started Harp Design Co., our initial plan was for me to take half the day to work on furniture, while Kelly took the other half to work on home goods, so that someone was always with the kids. Over the course of that summer, that plan had already dissolved. It turned out that I needed the whole day to develop the furniture we were designing. With little to do in regards to HDC, Kelly needed something of her own. At the time she dreamed aloud about returning to school, our house was still on the market and wasn't drawing many offers. My first thought—*Where will we get the money?*—was quickly followed by a second: *This is perfect.* If Kelly got a chance at a master's degree somewhere (and it would have to be on a full ride since we were broke) I figured dominoes would start to fall.

I recalled a spring break trip to New Orleans that I'd taken with my youth group during high school. One day, I found myself sitting next to my youth minister, Allen, whom I hero-worshiped. We were eating beignets at the famous Café Du Monde when he said this: "Clint, there are three types of people in this world. Those who make things happen. Those who watch things happen. And those who say, 'What just happened?' Also, Clint," he continued, "remember this: your integrity is the most important thing about you."

As Kelly made her announcement, I could practically taste the beignets and hear the words he'd spoken. I could also still hear what Paul had often told me: "Clint, nothing is really going to happen in your life until you put yourself in the position where things actually *have* to happen." Now I understood what they both meant. Kelly and I weren't just a couple of bystanders watching our lives happen. We had to actively craft our experience, one plank and one choice at a time. We couldn't predict what would happen, and God knows tough circumstances can befall any of us. But even then, we've got a say in how we respond—whether we'll become paralyzed or forge ahead. Chill out on the sidelines, and you get one kind of life. Charge out onto the field, roll around in the dirt, and do some fumbling, and you get another kind. We all get to choose.

"We have no money to pay for this," I finally said to Kelly, "but that's okay, because you'll definitely get a full ride somewhere."

She laughed and rolled her eyes, but I turned out to be right. A few weeks after she took the GRE and applied to a program in American studies at our old alma mater, an email arrived. "Dear Kelly," it read, "we are pleased to inform you that you have been accepted into the American studies graduate program at Baylor University on a full scholarship." And there it was. We were moving back to Waco.

*   *   *

After living in Houston for four years, we sold our home in October 2011—right at the tail end of the Great Recession. When we'd bought the place, we'd put down $20,000 and hoped to get that much back. But our buyers wouldn't budge on their offer, so we walked away with only $5,000 in equity. Ouch. That hurt the budget, because I still hadn't sold any tables and our savings were thin. But we agreed we weren't doing it for the money. We were on an adventure. We decided to take it.

A quick side note about money: Before I quit my job, we'd had many difficult conversations about possible consequences: bankruptcy, bad credit, home foreclosure, student loan default, car repossession—you name it—but in the end, we decided to go for our dream. I mean, is there ever really a good time to hang up your badge and start a business? When do we ever have enough money to do what we've always wanted to do? Kelly and I were at the point where we refused to make any more excuses. There'd always be car payments, a mortgage, and mouths to feed. "It's not your job to have all the answers," Paul would often remind me. "It's your job to go after what you truly and deeply feel you should be doing." That doesn't mean any of us should rush off half-cocked, with absolutely no plan or cash in place. A certain European misadventure had once taught me that painful lesson. But Kelly and I had a decent blueprint and around $25,000 in savings. Granted that money had to cover our bills and loans, car payments, a trip to New York City for my sister's wedding, a move to Waco, and anything that was needed to build our business. But I figured, even if I sold absolutely nothing, we could make it stretch for six months, maybe even eight. Ultimately we were willing to face any harsh financial realities that would likely arise if our plan went south. Every one of us has a unique financial picture that would make such a leap either sensible or senseless, depending on the circumstance. But in our case, it was time to jump. And jump we did.

Just before Christmas 2011, we moved into a tiny two-bedroom apartment in Waco, close to Baylor's campus. The plan was for me to rent a shop where I could bang together some tables while Kelly settled into her studies. We lived off a combination of our savings and my wife's $1,200-a-semester stipend. While I looked around town for a workshop I could afford, I decided to volunteer for Habitat for Humanity.

Why Habitat? My grandmom Martin, my mother's mom, had, in a way, led me toward it long after she'd passed away. She'd once worked for former president Jimmy Carter at the Carter Presidential Library in Atlanta. When the place first opened, I got to be there and even took pictures with the former president, who has since spent countless volunteer hours with Habitat and has championed its mission over his lifetime. I was around eleven or twelve at the time, with those buckteeth and a bad crew cut. I will always have a fond place in my heart for Jimmy Carter and his wife, Rosalynn. They cared for my beloved grandmother. When she retired, they threw her a huge party at the library and my family attended. Years down the road, as my grandmother lay on what we thought would be her deathbed, her old friend gave her a call to say good-bye. She got so excited when she heard the president was on the phone that she immediately rose from her hours-long nap and almost broke my cousin's wrist as she ripped the receiver from his hands. As if bolstered by his and Mrs. Carter's good wishes, my grandmother rebounded and lived a few months more.

I swear I could hear my grandmother telling me from the other side to go and volunteer for Habitat in Waco. I figured that in addition to getting involved in a worthy cause, I'd stay busy honing the very skills I'd need for building furniture, so that's exactly what I did when we moved to Waco. As Kelly dived deeper into her studies, I volunteered like it was my full-time job. I was building houses. I was working with tools. I was digging pipe trenches with inmates from a women's prison just outside of town. I was getting to know people. And all the while, I felt as if I were getting closer to something. I just didn't know what that something was.

Trouble is, volunteering doesn't pay very well. We were running out of money as the haunting questions mounted: Would I ever be able to find an affordable shop to rent? When would I start building furniture? Would Kelly have to take on a part-time job at a community college to help keep us afloat? Some days, my brain was in overdrive, chewing on the low moments from my past: the scarce funds and pillar-to-post existence of my childhood; the music career I'd never gotten off the ground; the lean days of scrubbing toilets in St. Petersburg; the decision to leave Paris after our money ran dry. How familiar our current situation felt.

Here we were, in the city where we'd first met, falling behind again in every conceivable way. As the pressure mounted, I felt like I was about to suffocate. I couldn't turn off the reeling thoughts and the feeling that I was about to drive us into another ditch. Then came the day when, in tears, I called my wife from the lot of that pink house, the place Kelly had spotted during our first days in Waco. For us, that ramshackle home had come to symbolize the bold, courageous dreamers we were, which is why I'd gone there in my lowest moment. I was trying to hold on to our bold, courageous dream. And then, less than an hour later, during a chance encounter at a gas station with a guy named Chip, the insane journey we'd been on took a dramatic and unexpected turn.

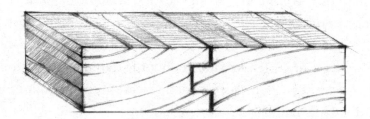

CHAPTER 9

In the Groove

When I got serious about making tables, my granddad gave me some advice. "If you've got a table saw," he told me, "you can make just about anything." He had me get a dado blade, which is a stacked blade system for a table saw that allows you to cut a thicker groove, or dado, in whatever you're cutting. Say you have a board that's 1 inch thick. If you run it on its edge over a half-inch stacked dado blade, you'll have a half-inch groove running down the length of the board. Flip the same board on its face and run the opposite edge over the dado blade on both sides, and you'll be left with a tongue. The same thing can be accomplished using a router with tongue-and-groove bits. It's a great feeling when those boards snap together just right. Everything fits. All the chaos that was once laid out on the floor is now taking shape. Tongue-and-groove all your boards and then join them together with glue and clamps. A tabletop is born.

The afternoon I met Chip at the gas pump, we chatted for ten minutes or so while our tanks filled up. Then he noticed Kelly and the kids in our SUV. "Listen, take your family home and come back to my shop so we can talk some more." he told me. I agreed and hopped back in the car. Kelly had figured out who I was talking to, and of course knew about my previous blown and unreturned voicemail, so she was immediately hopeful.

Soon after I dropped the family at home, I met Chip at their
office over on Bosque Boulevard—an old Craftsman style house,
turned into a workspace, that was the original Magnolia shop. I
walked in to find an empty meeting space. A young lady, who I'd
later learn was one of Joanna's design assistants, appeared from
around the corner.

"Hi, I'm Kristen," she said. "Can I help you?"

"Yeah, I'm Clint," I told her. "I just met Chip at a gas station
and he said to come here and we could talk for a bit."

"Right!" she said. "Okay, great. Hmmm. Just give me a second
and I'll see if I can find him. What was your name again?"

"Clint," I said. "Like Clint Eastwood."

Moments later, Chip appeared. "Hey, bud!" he said. "Come
hop in my truck and we'll drive around for a bit."

That ride was the shortest three hours of my life. We talked nonstop as he drove all around town, showing me some of the houses
he and Joanna—or "Jo-Jo," as he affectionately called her—had
already flipped. He also showed me others they hoped to renovate.
He even took me to a housing development he was in the middle
of constructing, which was a whole new kind of project for him
and his wife. And in between each stop, we connected. About our
families. Our lives up to then. Our dreams going forward.

"Jo-Jo has been wanting to add a furniture line to her home
goods offerings for a while now," he told me as we finally pulled into
the back lot of his shop and parked. "I think she tried before with
another guy, but it didn't work out. The furniture was great, but
I'm not even sure he's building anymore. You never know, man. I'm
sure she'd love to talk to you." Then he invited our family to dinner.

Sounded good to me. At this point, I didn't have a single client.
In fact, with our finances looking so bleak I'd even started toying
with the idea of looking into a full-time paid job on the Habitat

team. But now it looked like other possibilities might be sparking up. The following Wednesday, when we entered the front door of the Gaineses' ranch house, it was clear these two had talent and style. The place, which they'd renovated themselves, was gorgeous. "Come on in, guys!" Chip said, ushering us into the entryway.

All the kids ate first and then rushed out back to play. That left us four grown-ups sitting at the table over heaping helpings of pasta and marinara. We talked for a good uninterrupted forty minutes, which started with a round of "Do you know so-and-so?" In Waco, everybody is connected. Talk to someone long enough, and there's no doubt you'll find an acquaintance in common, or maybe even learn you were in the same class together back at Baylor. After a few minutes of that game—and after realizing we had some acquaintances in common—we got down to business.

I filled Joanna in on what Chip already knew: I'd quit my job in Houston so Kelly and I could start our own little furniture company. We hadn't yet sold any pieces, but we knew we eventually would. And that's when Joanna asked me the one question that changed the game, a question that would become a precursor to a similar conversation we'd end up having over and over again: "Clint, do you think if I drew up some designs on a piece of paper, you could possibly build them?"

You already know I said yes. What you don't know yet is what she asked me next. "You've mentioned pallets and reclaimed wood a bunch," she said. "Are the tables going to look like they were once pallets? Because if it's okay with you, I'd prefer they didn't."

"They won't, I promise," I said, assuring her that I could build her just about anything. Never mind that there were a grand total of four tables in my Harp Design Co. portfolio. And never mind that all my tools were in storage, and that we'd hauled none of the wood I'd gathered in Houston with us. And of course, I didn't have a shop . . . minor detail. "Just give me a bit of time to get some wood together," I told her. As I spoke, a slew of memories came rushing back: Me pulling apart old pallets in the garage for hours at a time. The sweat lodge. The wood-floor tabletop design. Notes in my sketchpad as I tried to figure out how to make those pallets look like tables and nothing else.

"Oh, and I'd love for one of the tables to have turned legs," she continued. "Could you do that?"

"Yeah, sure," I said. "I could make a farm table with a turned leg. I can do that."

Only tiny problem: I didn't really know how to use my lathe yet. At all.

The next day, when I went back to my volunteer job at Habitat, I knocked on the door of the director, John Alexander.

John had been overseeing Waco's chapter of Habitat since 1998. I'm sure he saw me as a bit of a mystery. I seemingly showed up out of nowhere, worked Monday through Friday for months without pay, could pretty much handle whatever was thrown at me on the jobsite (thank you, Granddad Martin), and talked on my lunch breaks about one day building furniture. "Hey, Clint," he'd shouted up at me once when I was on a ladder trimming the front of a house. "Do you live off a trust fund or something?" I laughed so hard I nearly fell to the ground, then yelled down, "Definitely no trust fund!"

John and I had gotten closer since then, and seeing as he now had a better appreciation of my finances and lack thereof, I felt comfortable asking him if he knew of an affordable garage or even a storage unit with electricity I could use to set up shop.

He thought for a minute, then said, "We do have a place over on Fifteenth Street, just down the road less than a mile from here. It's actually the original Habitat cabinet shop. Some Habitat homeowners and I got together and built it with our own hands. It's about 1,600 square feet and it's got all the electrical you'd need to build furniture. What if we rented that to you?"

I did the math in my head. Kelly and I had learned, when looking at homes around Waco, that you could expect to be in for about $1 per square foot for rent, which would make this place a minimum of $1,600 a month. And I figured a commercial space might run even more. But I played along.

"Wow, that sounds amazing," I said. "Um, how much would you want for it?"

He thought for a moment. "How about this, Clint? We're phasing it out and I don't want it to just sit there unoccupied. How does twenty-five dollars a month sound?"

The first thing that ran through my head was *Well, that's the top of my budget, but if you're sure!* But what came out of my mouth was something more along the lines of "Are you serious?" He was. I couldn't thank him enough.

John and I agreed I'd be responsible for the rent, electricity, and water. As I thanked him for his generosity, I remember wondering if I could bring my own water from home and pee out back to keep a lid on the water bill. Yes, we were that poor. But I now had a shop and my first client—and no clue whatsoever about how everything would come together. But clearly something was happening, and I kept moving forward.

As it goes in life, so it goes with carpentry. While you may start out with an idea and plan for how you're going to build something, it doesn't always end up that way. You don't have the pieces you need. You saw a few boards too short. Your day doesn't go as expected and the three hours you thought you'd have to spend in the shop turn out to be less than one. And yet you keep building. Keep hammering. Keep chiseling. Because if you sit around and wait for all the pieces to line up—for all the conditions to be perfect—you won't make it very far. And you certainly won't be able to finish six pieces of furniture by yourself in barely two months.

*   *   *

A week or so after our dinner with the Gaineses, I called Chip to let him know I had a shop. I'd discovered it was right next door to this tall, dilapidated white farmhouse turned crack house, but whatever. At least I had a place. Chip quickly volunteered to pick me up in his truck and help me get my tools out of storage. He dropped me back at the shop and left me with an "All right. Get to work, bud."

For the first few days, I went around town in search of pallets. Same song and dance from my Houston days, and I even got lucky again. As I drove down Valley Mills Drive, straight through the heart of town, I spotted a huge stack of pallets from the lumberyard of a building supply company. Bonus: The pallets looked like they were at least eight feet long! I went inside and asked if I could take some off their hands, and to my delight, they obliged. What I thought was eight feet turned out to be twelve feet of 1x4 boards nailed to four 3x3 posts. Bingo: I could make legs out of those.

When I agreed to make Jo some pieces, I just left out the part about how I really didn't know how to use the lathe I'd purchased back in Houston. Knowing her now, she probably wouldn't have cared and still placed an order, but my own insecurities egged on my silence. Before deciding to buy a lathe, I'd royally screwed up the legs on the first table prototype I'd shown Kelly. "I love the top!" she'd exclaimed. "But tell me about the base. There's sort of an Asian-fusion thing going on, and while that's cool, it's not the look I thought we were going for." That's when I decided I needed to buy the $319 lathe I'd seen advertised at a local discount tool store. Not only did I purchase the lathe, but I also forked over another $70 for turning chisels. I'll always remember standing in the checkout line with my kids, who saw me as their hero, while I was thinking about how I was completely gambling away their futures. After putting together my new lathe, I went on YouTube and found a video of a wood turner making a small honey dipper—it's what came up first when I googled "how to use a lathe." I stood there in my garage watching that video a few times. I put some thirty-inch-long, 4x4 stock on the lathe and turned it, doing my best to mimic the guy in the video. (Incidentally, this is also the way I'd learned to pick on my guitar back in junior high—simply by repeatedly watching close-ups of James Taylor's hands during a PBS concert.) When I was done, my sample turning looked like crap, but I was still proud. I then attempted to make four incredibly simple legs and hoped they looked similar. I replaced the original Asian-fusion base with those four legs and wasn't too impressed with myself. I hadn't used the lathe again since.

Now, with my bounty of pallets sticking out from the back of the SUV, I returned to my new shop. I pulled out my trusty hammer and small pry bar. My tools were no match for those bad boys. Instead of the short but sturdy nails that had held together the pallets I'd been working with back in Houston, these boards had been hammered together with legit 16-penny nails. Lots of them. I ran to the store and bought a four-pound sledgehammer and crowbar. It was backbreaking work. Day after day, I carefully pulled those pallets apart, doing my best to salvage every foot while removing all the nails. Turn a piece of wood with a nail in it on your lathe and watch how fast your chisels get ruined. I couldn't afford to break my tools. I even used a pair of pliers and a drill to surgically remove certain stubborn nails. It felt like a strange breed of dentistry.

By the time Joanna showed up a few days later with the sketches she promised, it actually looked like something was happening in my shop. I had a pile of wood in the middle of the floor, like dirty laundry. My few tools were set up and the sturdy worktable I'd made from the scaffolding planks I found in the Houston construction site trash heap was sitting to the side. "Hey, can I buy this one?" Joanna asked when she spotted it. "Sorry, can't sell it," I said, laughing (while also crying a little on the inside as I could've used the cash). "Too many memories of the crazy ride Kelly and I have been on. But I can't tell you how happy it makes me that you like it."

She handed me her basic sketches, which included a couple of dining room tables, a coffee table, a bench, and a rolling island.

"What do you think of these?" she asked.

I glanced at the sheet. "This looks good," I told her. "You got it."

"Awesome!" she said. "How long do you think it'll take you?"

I shrugged. "I don't know," I said. "Maybe a few weeks?"

"That's great," she said. "As a matter of fact, at the beginning of May, I'll be having a sale in my house of a bunch of home goods. I'd love to have everything ready to sell by then."

I agreed. That would give me two months. Joanna said she'd swing back by in a week to check on everything. Then as she walked out, she looked back over her shoulder and yelled out, "And, Clint, don't forget about the turned-leg farm table, okay?"

Crap.

*   *   *

Our money was almost gone. All the bills I'd been paying down before I quit my job were still there. Toss in the cost of that New York City trip, our relocation expenses, the new tools and materials

I'd purchased, pre-K for Hudson, medical bills for Holland's birth, and other debts, and you can see why we were at the edge. And that one credit card we had? Totally maxed out.

What's funny is that when I considered telling John Alexander that his price for renting the shop was at the top of our budget, it actually was. At that point, we had less than a thousand dollars left in savings and were close to running out of Kelly's graduate school stipend. But at least one thing was going my way: I had secured a place to get cranking on Joanna's tables. Now all I had to do was dust off my lathe and figure out how to turn a leg.

CHAPTER 10

Leg Work

*Turning a leg on the lathe can be therapeutic. I, like every
other turner out there, have my own unique style, from the
way I hold the chisels to the way I pass them over the wood.
When I turn, a few things have to be in place. One, I've got
to have my music. Switching it on is like throwing a magical cloak over myself and disappearing from the concerns of
the world. I have all the blanks prepped and ready usually
stacked next to the lathe, which means I've cut them all to
length with a centering hole poked on each end. This way, I
can keep turning without having to walk away from the lathe
to prepare more stock. After my first cuts, I then use skews,
parting tools, bowl gouges, and other chisels to give the leg
the shape I want it to have. It's in this process of creating legs,
candlesticks, bowls, and other turned objects that I experience
the reality that a furniture maker is really an artist. Like a
potter covered in clay after a day's work, we builders go home
with splinters in our palms, sawdust under our nails, and
satisfaction in our hearts that we've handcrafted a piece that
will forever tell a story.*

In the days after Joanna stopped by the shop, we exchanged a few
text messages to clarify details about how she wanted her pieces to
look. Then a few more treasure hunts through the city landed me

some amazing lumber for the job. All good, until I tried to turn the legs for the farm table.

I'd been avoiding the task, mainly because I didn't know how to tackle it. But time was running out. Joanna was expecting the pieces to be ready by early May, and it was already mid-April. I had to make a start. I plugged a blank into the lathe, then measured down about four and a half inches from the top of the leg and made a line. I left that part of the leg stock straight so I'd have enough room to attach the skirt. Below that line, I rounded out the rest of the stock. After it was nice and cylindrical, I got creative: I cut in here, rounded out there, and on and on I went down the length of the leg. Four hours later, I'd finished just one leg. And by the time I reached the bottom of the leg, I'd already forgotten how I did the turnings up at the top.

I was a wreck. *If one leg took me four hours*, I kept thinking, *how in the world will any of this ever be profitable? And how can I re-create a leg when I can't even recall how I turned it?* Common sense should've told me to take a breath and realize that I was still learning and would improve with practice. And down the line, I could make easier styles. But when you're feeling as stressed and scared as I was, common sense isn't all that common. I'd promised to make a table that I now felt was completely out of my reach. I sanded the leg I'd made, took it off the lathe, and crawled home.

I showed the leg to Kelly. "It's great!" she said. And then she spotted my drooping shoulders. "What's wrong?" she asked.

"Working on that leg reminds me of just how little I know about what I'm doing," I told her. Before she could respond, Hudson and Holland came down the stairs.

"Hey, Daddy, what's that?" asked Hudson, noticing the leg I held.

"Just something I was working on at the shop."

"Can we have it?" he asked.

"Sure," I told him. "Just be careful taking it upstairs."

My two kids marched happily up the staircase with their new-found treasure, and I spent the rest of the night in a daze.

The next morning, when I came downstairs before heading back to the shop, the kids were already up and running around. On our table sat the turned leg. It was now adorned with stickers. "Awesome!" read one. "Great job!" read another. "We love you, Dad!" said one near the bottom. Hudson and Holland had put every sticker they could find on that piece of wood.

I held back the tears. It was the sweetest thing. Was I inspired to go and start turning more legs? Well, no. But I was reminded that I had my family in my corner, and that Kelly and the kids supported and loved and believed in me, and it was just what I needed. I went to the shop that day, propped that leg covered with stickers in a corner where I could see it, and got back to work.

A week or so later, Joanna came by the shop to check on my progress. I was knee-deep in building by then, and things had finally started to come together.

"What's that over there, Clint?" she asked. She was pointing at my disastrous attempt at a farm table leg. "Did you make that?"

"What? That leg?" I said. "Oh yeah, that's just something I was practicing on. It didn't really turn out like I wanted. But Kelly and the kids liked it. See the stickers?"

"Yeah," she said, "and I love it, too. In fact, that's the one. I want you to use that for the farm table. Can you make it again?"

"I mean, yeah, I think so," I said. "If not, then I guess we're both in trouble."

Insert awkward laugh here.

*   *   *

As I continued to chip away at Joanna's order, Kelly pressed along in school, and our kids attended a mother's day out program three days each week. We were happy to be in Waco, happy to live somewhere familiar. We were still broke as hell, but nonetheless glad about our choice to relocate.

With our apartment so close to Baylor, we'd often stroll over to campus and let our kids play on the grounds we'd once walked as students. They loved it. The campus was the biggest backyard we'd ever had, complete with a real-live bear (the Baylor mascot) that we could visit and say hello to if we ever got bored. Even so, after a few months in the tight quarters of our apartment, we knew we'd eventually have to move. At two a.m. on many nights, we were awakened by the sound of thumping music courtesy of the students who lived next door. "Can you please keep the noise down a little?" I'd stumble over and ask, wearing athletic shorts, black tube socks, and a T-shirt. Just over a decade earlier, we would've been those very students causing a commotion. Now, Kelly and I were two thirtysomethings with kids, a fledgling business, and an intense study schedule. We needed our shut-eye.

Sleep, however, would have to wait, because Kelly and I wanted to have another child. Years earlier, when we were engaged, we'd talked about wanting a big family. But after Kelly had the emergency C-section with Hudson, we'd been advised that three should be our limit. Three became our goal. We also wanted our kids to be relatively close in age so they could grow up together. With Hudson already five and Holland two, we decided it was about time to go for a third. Yes, even with Kelly in grad school. Even with me trying to get the business going. And even with the two kids we already had requiring just about every ounce of energy we could give. "I know it doesn't make any sense and I have no idea how we'll make it work," Kelly had admitted, "but it just feels like we should try." A month later, Kelly was pregnant.

Neck-deep in school and work and with a new baby on the way, we had little time for making friends around town. Finding a church probably would've helped, but we couldn't muster the desire to go there yet. Honestly, with all the upheaval and moving around, we hadn't consistently gone to church since that year I'd worked part-time as a pastor in Houston. My personal spiritual journey continued to be all over the map. By the time we moved to Waco, God had become more a mystery to me than ever before—a beautiful, terrifying, creative, and wonderful mystery I didn't want to solve. I was okay with not knowing how God worked, and not having all the answers. It was enough for me to jump out into a mysterious unknown and trust that a greater power was in control.

*　　*　　*

All through April, I kept building. I finally got the hang of turning legs and the tables started coming together. May rolled around and the home sale with Joanna was coming up. In the days before my deadline, I worked around the clock, trying to get it all done: building, sanding, staining, painting, distressing, finishing, gluing, turning, sweating, bleeding, and sometimes even tearing up. It was a roller coaster. The day before the sale arrived and I still had stuff left to do. *It's now or never*, I kept telling myself. By noon that day, it became clear it was going to be a very long night.

I drove home at five p.m., ate dinner with Kelly and the kids, and then went back up to the shop. Kelly wasn't too excited about me being there so late, given the crack house, with its steady stream of customers, right next door. But I promised her I'd lock myself in. And frankly, it's not like we had another option. Around midnight, I flipped a seven-foot farm table over to paint the underside. On the way down, it slipped out of my hands and slid right down my entire shin, shaving off a giant chunk of flesh as it went. I groaned, wrapped a shop rag around it, and kept going. I worked till six the next morning with a throbbing, bloody leg, then went home and lay down on the floor and took a nap. At seven a.m., the kids came downstairs and jumped on my stomach. It was time to deliver my items.

I took a quick shower and wrapped up my leg, then jumped back in the car and returned to the shop. There in the center of the floor sat the six pieces I'd completed: three tables, including the farm table with turned legs; a rolling island on large casters; a bench; and a coffee table. I couldn't fit much in my car, so trip after trip, I lugged the items over to Joanna's house. I set up most of the tables outside on the front lawn. "Looking good!" said Joanna from the house. *Exhale.* By the time I showed up with the island on the third of five trips, customers were already arriving. I finished my deliveries, went home, and collapsed.

The next morning, Joanna called. "We sold it all, Clint!" she told me. "I even got orders for a couple more pieces. Nice work, bud!" The furniture sales brought in around $5,000, which we'd agreed to split down the middle. That $2,500 was the first money I'd made in over a year. And the farm table with the turned legs? It went quick. In fact, over the next few years, the very leg that I'd once perceived as a complete failure would become the signature design I'd use on table after table. To this day, that leg, covered in my kids' stickers, sits in my shop, reminding me that the first leg of a race doesn't have to define the last.

*   *   *

In the months following that first order with Joanna, she called me pretty consistently, asking for farm tables and benches and islands. At one point, she even bought space at a local store and displayed my furniture there with her home goods. Not a single piece sold. It all just sat there for months, collecting dust. That's how things sometimes go in sales: feast or famine, neither of which is predictable.

Good thing I began receiving calls from other clients. A church down in Austin got ahold of me through our friend Jaclyn back in Houston. One of the leaders there wanted me to build a hutch that would sit at the back of the sanctuary, as well as a wall cabinet that would house name tags. I had never built a hutch or a cabinet, but you know me: I entertain every possibility. To discuss the details, the church leaders set up a conference call that would include me and three other people.

"Hi, Clint, it's Elizabeth," the call began. "I also have Dan and Bill on the line. Dan is a professor with his Ph.D. in physics, and Bill is an engineer. Both do woodworking on the side and wanted to be a part of this project. I'll let them explain what we want."

Oh dear God. Why in the world were they calling me, then? That opener alone was enough to give me a panic attack, but I played along. Over the next twenty minutes, they described what they had in mind, and I scribbled notes. Before we signed off, I agreed to give them a price in the next few days.

For a carpenter or any other kind of artisan, pricing your own work is one of the most complicated parts of the job. Price it too high, and it may seem that you think you're Picasso. If your client accepts a high price, it's no surprise when his or her expectation level is sometimes off the charts to match that price. On the other hand, price your work too low, and you won't be able to afford to eat. And while your client will likely be grateful to get such a killer deal, and probably won't be too picky in the end, he or she will spread the word about your low price and you'll be inundated with orders for complicated pieces for pitiful pay. It's a real challenge.

I did my best to figure out a price. I wanted to get it just right so I wouldn't have a physics professor and an engineer breathing down my neck. I didn't know yet that they would turn out to be two incredibly kind and relatable people with fair expectations, nothing like my projection of them, but that's what fear does: it turns you into a crazy person. Anyway, after talking it over with Kelly, I decided to quote on the higher side. Swallowing hard, I told them, "I can do it for two thousand dollars total." The whole time I was thinking, *Am I really asking someone to pay me thousands when I've never made more than seven hundred dollars for one piece?* For me, that was a giant leap. And it's one I'm glad I dared to take, because the potential clients said yes at once. I couldn't believe it.

Not long after, I found the greatest pallets ever: Kelly and I got reacquainted with the Ogdens, old Waco friends from our Baylor days who happened to own an industrial belting company. The pallets their raw materials were shipped on were constructed of six-foot-long oak and pecan boards. I let the church know I'd make the hutch and cabinet out of this lumber. They loved the idea. When it was all said and done, I delivered the pieces to Austin half proud of what I'd created and half surprised I had actually pulled it off. My clients were pleased and my confidence was bolstered.

As more orders for tables and custom work trickled in, we were still living in our cramped apartment. With Kelly pregnant, the thought of three kids in a small two-bedroom gave us both hives.

"Clint, I know this is going to sound crazy," Kelly told me one afternoon when she came home from class, "but I think I've found a house I want."

"Like, to rent?" I asked

"No, like, to buy," she said.

"Yes, you're right," I told her. "That does sound crazy."

"Hear me out," she said. "It's a little white cottage close to Castle Heights, not far from here. It has a 'For Sale' sign out front. I think we could renovate it and make it so cute!"

As an aside, we never bought that pink house in Waco we'd once daydreamed of renovating. Sure, we'd been bold enough to give the Realtor a call, but except for Kelly's mutual fund from her grandmother (which we had strictly agreed would not be bail-out cash but rather saved for an investment as her grandmother had wished), we had no money. Maybe, we reasoned, if we could find someone crazy enough to give us a loan, we could use the mutual fund as a down payment. We gave the Realtor a seriously lowball offer, something like $45,000. That got us nowhere with the owners, so we had to pass. Yet in the end, that pink house more than served its purpose for us. And when the little white cottage appeared on our radar, we jumped out on a limb once again, this time knowing we were being led somewhere great even if we didn't know where.

"Well," I said, "Chip was telling me the other day that we should buy a house. He even has a banker he'd introduce us to. Honestly, what he was saying made sense, when you consider how much we're paying in rent. Then again, I'm not sure anyone would loan us money. But why not give it a shot?"

Chip's friend Joe Nesbitt had worked with the Gaineses for several years as they bought and sold houses all around town, which had to have been much easier to do in those prerecession days. A Baylor grad and Waco native, Joe loved the idea of people investing in his beloved city. "You won't find an easier person to work with," Chip told me as he gave me Joe's number. The next day, I called Joe up and asked if he could help us get a home loan.

Joe is an amazing guy—big personality, insanely dry sense of humor, and a great heart. "I'd love to help you!" he said right away. "Let's do it! I'll tell you what. I'll have my assistant email you a loan app. You fill that out and we'll go from there."

Right. A loan app. Welp, there goes that idea, I thought. But I filled it out anyway. I'll always remember this on the form:

Total Cash Amount in Checking Account(s): $615

Total Cash Amount in Savings Account(s): $0

The one bright spot on that application was the $12,000 mutual fund from Kelly's grandmother. That was it. I filled out the form with our car loan information, my student loan, how much we paid in rent, and the amounts we owed on our credit cards (we now had a second one that was almost maxed out). I laughed out loud and shook my head skeptically as I hit "send" on the email.

A couple of days later, Joe called. "Hey, Clint," he said. "I got all your info, and you should put an offer on that house right away, okay? We're gonna make this happen, bud. Go get 'em!"

I was beyond shocked. I called Kelly and we both freaked out. We couldn't believe it. I texted Chip to say thanks and after that called the Realtor. A couple of weeks later, we were under contract. For a solid month after we closed I ripped into that house, trying my best to pull off Kelly's design plan. She and the kids would bring lunch and dinner over and we'd have a picnic. From that tiny backyard, we'd stare at our little house and feel like it was a castle.

On the weekend of July Fourth, we moved into our 1,390-square-foot home with two bedrooms, one bathroom, and a closed-in side porch that we would turn into a third bedroom. We were thrilled. Over the next five years, Joe Nesbitt, through many other projects, would cement his place in our "People We Couldn't Have Done This Without" Hall of Fame. He was a part of the miracle, among so many others.

Some years totally transform the playing field. For us, 2012 was that year. We'd started by relocating to Waco to chase a crazy dream. By March, I'd made an incredible connection at a *gas station*, landed my very first customer, and opened a shop. Before the start of summer, I'd learned to turn a leg and somehow sold six pieces, along with that hutch and cabinet for the church in Austin. And at year's end, Kelly and I received a gift far greater than all of those events combined. A week before Christmas, Camille Harp kicked her way into the world. Named after my father's mother, that little angel would be our second girl and the beloved closing punctuation mark on our family.

But a few months before we welcomed Camille—and just when we thought our year couldn't get any more insane—Joanna stopped by my shop with an announcement that would turn everything on its head.

CHAPTER 11

Varying Grits

Use the right grit of sandpaper, and you're gold. Use the wrong grit, and it can kick you in the pants by creating more work. When I first started building, for instance, I used 60 grit on everything: hardwood, soft wood, new or old, 60 grit was my leadoff batter. By the time I got to applying stain, I would find little swirly sanding marks all over my tabletop and be screaming at the carpentry gods for once again foiling my hard work. Thanks to a chat with my woodworking brother-in-law, Jonty, I changed my ways. The grits you choose will vary depending on the type of wood you're working with. If you're sanding a rough piece with deep grains, you might start with 60-grit sandpaper, which essentially means the paper has 60 abrasive particles per square inch. You might even pull out the belt sander and use 36 grit, which is even more intense. Or maybe you want to leave all those glorious marks and that wonderful character, so you skip straight to 120 or 150, or better yet to 220, in order to clean it up a bit, to knock off some splinters without getting rid of all the natural character the wood displays. It's a tricky dance. But when you use the correct grit, you can make a piece of wood do whatever you want it to do.

"Hey, Clint, how's it going?" Joanna said as she walked into my shop.

"It's good," I said. "Busy for sure. What about you? What's up in the Gaineses' world?"

157

"Oh, you know," she said. "Things are crazy as always. Actually, I got an email from this guy the other day. He said he'd seen a blog post about me on a national design blog called *Design Mom*. My friend Molly Winn [a local photographer who'd become a friend of ours as well] had submitted pictures to the blog, and they ended up doing a cool write-up on me. Anyway, this guy who reached out, he works for a TV production company out of Colorado. And he wants to develop an idea for a possible show to pitch to HGTV."

On the outside, I played it cool: a subtle smile accompanied by some heartfelt well-wishes. But on the inside, I was running around in circles with my hair on fire. *What!?!! You've got to be kidding me! OH. MY. LORD. YES! You guys are going to kill it! And if you need a carpenter . . . I mean . . . Hi! . . .*

"Wow, Jo, that is so awesome!" I said. "Congratulations."

After that conversation, it was a waiting game. And a game of survival. Although we were making a bit of money from the projects I'd taken on, we still had kids to feed and bills mounting. Kelly's stipend had run out and we knew she wouldn't get another; she'd decided to step away from her studies to take care of new-born Camille and invest time in our growing small business. We also now owned a house that came with a mortgage. Things were as tight as ever, and we started to wonder if we'd made the right move. And in the back of my mind sat the possibility that Joanna had put on the table. She might one day have her own television show on HGTV, and I could maybe, just maybe, build her some pieces for that show. Part of me knew it was a long shot: there was no telling whether she'd even get the show, or if she'd want me on it. But another part of me, a much bigger part, was hoping. Meanwhile, Chip and Jo worked with the production company to create a sizzle reel—a ten-minute promo video that served as a snapshot of the show being pitched.

Whenever Joanna would stop by the shop, she'd give me updates: "Yeah, we're still waiting to hear" or "I got an email saying the person who makes the decision is out of town" or "They won't have their meeting on new show ideas for a few weeks." The waiting game was tough for me, so it must've been excruciating for Chip and Joanna. As Kelly and I would discover years later, television was one of those industries where you put yourself out there and then leave it all in the hands of people who are looking at a hundred other ideas that are not always that much different from yours—and you sit by the phone.

Until one day, seemingly out of nowhere, you get an answer. "Clint," Joanna told me one afternoon, "they liked our sizzle reel and they want to do a pilot!" And then, as she turned to go, she casually uttered the sentence that blew me away: "You ready to build some tables on TV?"

I called Kelly as soon as Joanna left the shop. "Not only are they going to make a pilot," I told her, "but Jo has invited me to be in it!"

It was surreal. The pilot—tentatively titled *Fixer Upper*—would feature Chip and Joanna as they remodeled a home from top to bottom for a client in the Waco area. Somewhere in the midst of tearing down walls, designing, and tiling bathrooms and back-splashes, Jo would need me to build something. What she'd need, I had no idea—something big, something small, or maybe even multiple somethings. Regardless of what she asked of me, I would just have to do what I always did—figure it out.

*   *   *

As they counted down to the start of filming, Joanna and I kept working. We hammered out a style for her farmhouse look and sold it to anyone who would buy it. Without thinking about it, we established the designer-builder relationship that would one day be on display for the world to see. Some of our ideas worked, some didn't, but we forged ahead. I collected pallets all around Waco and dragged them back to my shop, piecing together as many farm tables as I could. With sales picking up a bit, I bought an affordable single-axle ten-foot trailer to haul my pallet discoveries.

It was during these months that some of my fondest memories with the Gaineses were made. There was the time Kelly, Chip, Joanna, and I sat in my shop with all our kids eating sandwiches from a local Waco favorite, Schmaltz's Sandwich Shoppe. We were all kind of quiet, just wondering what in the world we were all getting into and how it was all going to work out. There were the times Chip and I went to lunch and just talked about how crazy it was to even have the chance at a pilot episode, and that if it worked, great, but if not, well, we'd be okay.

And there was the time when Chip and Jo were deciding whether to buy a farmhouse in the country just outside of town. Chip and Jo, as I'd come to learn, didn't say no to a challenge very often. Being someone who loves a good ol'-fashioned challenge myself, I can relate. As we sat there, Chip surprised me when he asked me—a guy who was still clearly trying to figure out his own life—for my opinion on the farmhouse.

"All I've thought about lately is what God might have us do with this whole farm thing," he said. "Just curious . . . what do you think?"

"Huh. I don't really know what you should do." I thought for a second. "But in my opinion . . . well . . . I don't think God cares. I really don't. I mean why would God care if you buy a farm? It's land and a house and money. I think God just cares if you try. I don't think God cares who wins football games, Grammy awards, or the Nobel Peace Prize, but I'm guessing God enjoys watching people pour everything into scoring a touchdown, writing a song, or taking humanity to the next level. So, yeah, go buy the farm if you really want to. And, hey, if it all blows up in your face, I think God will be in the front row giving you a standing ovation for trying. . . . I know I will."

Isn't it great when you're talking to someone in a way that you hope they'd talk to you? Not sure if Chip could tell, but I was dying for someone to say that to me. We can live a structured life that's within bounds, but there's also an option to go out and live a totally uncharted life. As far as we know, this is the only life we have. And when I sat and had lunch with Chip that day, it was clear I was only interested in making the most of that life.

And that life had come with plenty of surprises. I mean, what were the chances that a random producer would happen to run across a blog post featuring Joanna? And how did a guy like me, who didn't even know how to use a lathe until recently, get a shot at appearing on a national series? Nowadays, new shows seem to pop up all over the place; follow a few production companies on social media, and you'll hear about new pilot releases a few times a month. With Netflix, Amazon, Hulu, YouTube, and all the others, there's a new show around every corner and countless more in the idea stages. But back in 2011 when I quit my job—and before people were getting discovered on social media left and right—that wasn't the case. The possibility of a TV show was the last thing on my mind. I was busy setting up a quiet place in my garage with no lights, cameras, or people watching.

All that being said, the excitement of the pilot being filmed did light up the part of me that naturally gravitates toward entertaining. Up to that point, I'd spent much of my life in front of people. Whether taking on a starring role in a play or musical (which I did during high school), leading worship for ten people or two thousand with my acoustic guitar, acting in a short film, or even making presentations and forging connections for my previous sales jobs, I had so often been in the spotlight. And then I'd decided to shift from this public person into a solitary craftsman, toiling away to build furniture in his shop. Which consequently meant officially setting aside the biggest aspiration of my youth: pursuing a musical career.

My last musical hoorah had come after we'd returned from Paris and settled in Dallas. Kelly and I went to a Coldplay concert. I got us tickets right by the stage, and we could've sworn Chris Martin's sweat landed on our faces. It was glorious—everything I ever wanted in a concert. We left there and went to a late-night diner, where we sat and talked about how magical the experience had been, and how we wanted to live a life that felt magical. The next day, I went and bought a microphone and set up a small recording studio in our guest bedroom. I pulled out pen and paper and sat down to write some songs. Nothing came. In retrospect, it all makes perfect sense. Music wasn't supposed to be my path. But at the time, it was just so frustrating. I still had music in my veins, but it just wasn't flowing.

Over the next couple of years, I slowly let it go. I never got rid of my instruments, and you can still hear me singing in the shop just about any day I'm in there. But that journey had to come to an end for another one to begin. By the time I left my job in 2011, I had at last made peace with packing away my musical dream. Whether I'd miss playing music or performing more, I wasn't sure. But when I'd disappear into my garage alone, that's when the true work began: figuring out who I was and what I was supposed to be doing.

I was meeting regularly with my mentor, Paul, back then, and one afternoon, he called me with an assignment. "I'm going to send you this link," he told me. "It's the actor Ed Burns talking about his fears. Watch it when you get home, Clint. Replay it many times and let it sink in."

I watched it. Ed Burns looked straight at the camera and confessed that he wondered when everybody would figure out that he was a phony. When would he be revealed for what he truly was—a normal guy figuring out what the heck he was doing every day? It made more sense to me than just about anything I'd ever seen. I knew exactly what he was saying. It was almost as if I was listening to myself. For years, I'd tried to cover up the fact that I came from nothing. When you're wearing fire engine red sweatpants that are three sizes too small and nothing like the cool clothes that your classmates are sporting, it's hard to hide the fact that you don't have what everybody else has. But you still try to hide it. You get funnier. You get more sarcastic. You get nicer. When the cool guy, Patrick, is talking to other kids about his family ski trip, you chime in and say you've been skiing, too, when the closest you've ever gotten to a ski slope is sledding down the hill in your backyard on a trash can lid. You grab a guitar and fight like hell to rise above your situation. You tear a ligament in your elbow in the midst of JV baseball tryouts, go home and cut the end off the smallest sock you can find to make a cheap compression sleeve so you can still play. You fake it till you make it. You go to a college that's more expensive than anything you can remotely afford, borrowing nearly all of the $50,000 it costs, and just figure you'll somehow pay it off with money you can't see coming. You hustle in a medical sales job, hoping others don't see how much you hate what you're doing and, above all else, that no one asks you a serious medical question.

What *don't* you do? Reveal your true self. Ever. You don't let anyone get too close. You definitely don't bare your soul to a life coach over two years and finally open up to your wife about your biggest insecurities. You don't strip away all the facades you've put in place over the years, leaving yourself vulnerable to the judgments of everyone you know. And you don't walk away from the highest salary you've ever seen, go into the garage, and make furniture building your new full-time job.

Or maybe you do. Maybe you take a huge freakin' jump off the side of the cliff and leave that scared, miserable version of yourself far behind. And maybe, if the opportunity arises, you trade the solitude of your shop for the possibility of an upward trajectory.

From the moment Kelly and I learned there could be a pilot, we began discussing it nonstop. We had a million questions: What would this mean for our family and our company? Would I be able to sustain Harp Design Co. and be part of a show? Would one help or hurt the other? What would it feel like to build furniture with a camera on the sidelines, watching your every move? And how would being more widely recognized change things? Sometimes talking about it all was fun; other times, it made the waiting feel more excruciating.

Our conversations shifted on the day Joanna stopped by the shop with the news that the show was no longer theoretical. The pilot was happening. Kelly and I had no idea what any schedule might look like. We just knew that life was going to get crazier. That's when I recalled something Paul had often said to me: "Clint, all I can tell you is that one day, this journey will take on a life of its own," he'd told me after I'd quit my job. "And instead of sitting around wondering how in the world it will all work out, you'll find yourself hanging on for dear life." How right he would turn out to be.

*　　*　　*

As we looked ahead to the pilot's filming, a stark reality hit: even if this show worked out, we needed more money. And as I began to panic and even lose sight of going for my dream from behind the growing stack of bills, a regular paycheck seemed most logical. We had a third child on the way and a new mortgage. And sure, I had some clients here and there, but my earnings weren't anywhere close to what we needed. One day over dinner I announced to Kelly, "I've got to get a job." It was a tough realization for both of us, but it couldn't be ignored. I wasn't quite turning my back on my dream; it's just that I could only continue giving it my 100 percent if our basic needs were being met. Having some kind of cash flow would, in essence, allow me to plug away, little by little, at our small business venture while on a bit more stable ground.

The whole furniture-building thing was a great idea, but it didn't bring in enough money for me to provide for my family, and I found myself reverting to my old ways of thinking. *Get over it, Clint. Be a grown-up and do the responsible thing and find some work.* I set out on a search.

The whole time I looked around, I was worried that if and when a show was filmed, I'd end up missing the cut because I'd taken a job to keep the lights on. It was like suddenly having to go study right before the kickoff of your high school football championship game. *Too bad.* I had to make some dough.

At the time, Waco was showing signs of a small growth spurt, but there weren't too many job openings for an unemployed carpenter. My best bet, I figured, was some kind of position at Baylor. I dragged out my computer, updated my résumé, and submitted online applications for a handful of jobs. I'd done my best to re-craft my CV—a task I thought I'd never again have to do—and in a strange way, I felt hopeful. Maybe everything I'd done was somehow leading me to a wonderful position at a great university. My alma mater was growing fast, and working there could bring me a lot of opportunity, not to mention the possibility of reduced tuition for my kids one day. So I applied and waited for a response. I didn't get a single one. *Based on my grades there were probably alarms set to go off if I ever got within a phone call of the place.*

*   *   *

Now, if you're confused, know that I was, too. I had quit my job to go for my dream. But the realities were sinking in, and I was freaking out and desperately searching for a way out. Imagine a guy who knows the basics of swimming, who then tries to swim the English Channel with little training. After a couple of hundred yards the guy realizes, *Holy crap! I can't do this!* and starts to flail about, even forgetting how to float. That was me.

Around this time, my old friend John Alexander moved on from the fifteen years he'd spent building Waco Habitat. "It's time for a change," he told me when I dropped by to visit him. "I'm ready to explore new opportunities. But if you're interested, my job will be open." I walked back to my car with my head spinning. *Habitat? Yes! This is it! This is why I once felt like my grandmother was telling me from the other side of the grave to go and volunteer with Habitat—so I could one day become director.* I was absolutely convinced that this was the direction I should go in. Director of Habitat for Humanity Waco—it even sounded amazing. My grandmom would be so proud. I even came up with an idea for my first year there: I could add a furniture component to the equation. Habitat had scrap wood all over the place, and we could use those scraps to make tables for homeowners. It was perfect.

It was also in line with my original vision for Harp Design Co. In the beginning, I didn't just want to build furniture. I wanted to craft it and give it away. For every table I made, I hoped to donate another. Following in the footsteps of companies like TOMS shoes and Warby Parker, I envisioned launching a revolutionary furniture company. For a time, Kelly lovingly played along with my idea. But as I got incredibly close to making our company a nonprofit by filing a 401(c)3, my wife spoke up, and I finally heard her. Starting a 401(c)3 would come with too many restrictions. Kelly was right and we ultimately opted to launch, build, and sustain a for-profit company. We could still give away tables, and that's how we started. But, even though we had given away some furniture, the plan hadn't really worked out. Then, up from the ashes came the Habitat opportunity. If I got the director job, I could start my revolution there.

Except there was one tiny glitch: I didn't get the job.

As I contemplated my next steps, the conversations I'd had with Paul replayed in my head. Every time we sat down together I was always hoping he'd say something like, "Don't worry, Clint. It'll definitely come together. You're going to sell furniture and it'll be awesome." He never did. I should've known better than to expect concrete assurances from a man who jokingly described himself as an "agent of death." That name made more sense to me the longer we worked together. Paul was the equivalent of 36 grit on an industrial belt sander, the kind you don't want to touch while it's running unless you want to see bone. After I met Paul, the layers really started to come off. He helped me to shed a false version of myself—to kill off the pretense so the real me could show up.

In place of cheap promises, Paul let me sit with the fear. He let me wallow in it until it worked its way out of my soul. And along the way he'd continue to give me homework. I remember a film he told me to watch, *Touching the Void*. It was about a pair of mountain climbers who chose to scale one of the most dangerous peaks in South America. They were tied together so that if either one fell, the other could hopefully save him. As they climbed, the weather turned bad and one of the climbers slipped and tumbled down the mountainside. The other climber stuck himself in the side of the mountain with his crampons and held on for dear life. As he tried to pull up the fallen climber, both realized that it wasn't going to work. The problem was, they couldn't communicate about it: one climber was hanging off a cliff and the other was back up the mountain and beyond earshot. After what must've felt like an eternity, the climber who hadn't fallen made the incredibly difficult decision to cut his partner loose.

Once he cut the rope, his partner fell into a deep cavern. He somehow survived, landing on a ledge covered in thick snow attached to a wall of ice. He sat there. Confused. Scared. Weighing his options. With broken bones and his energy fading, scaling the sheer wall of ice above him wasn't possible. Lying there on the ledge till he died seemed even worse. With the rope he had left, he lowered himself down, descending even deeper into the darkness. Upon reaching the bottom of the cavern with literally just enough rope, he discovered a way out. After days of dragging himself through the snow and down the mountain, he found his way back to camp.

If that climber had sat there on the ledge, paralyzed by his fear, he would've lost his life. Instead, he lowered himself into the complete unknown. He wasn't even sure how deep the cavern went or if he had enough rope to reach the bottom. But he went for it. And because he did, he saved himself.

The point? Sitting on the ledge in my life was no longer an option. Sure, I was still yelling as loudly as I could to the top of the mountain to see if anybody could throw me a rope, but I refused to curl up and die. So I lowered myself, my wife, and our kids down a little deeper into the unknown, and I didn't look back. Well, okay, I did look back a few times. Actually, I was freaking out. I continued to stress and hope for a savior to rescue me from this seemingly bottomless cavern I was in, and I even contemplated quitting the whole journey and shutting down Harp Design Co. But all the while, my feet were reaching for solid ground. And in time, I was building a few woodworking projects for the *Fixer Upper* pilot, hoping my anxiety wouldn't be visible when the camera was finally pointed at me.

PART THREE

JOURNEYMAN

When we build, let us think that we build forever. Let it not be for present delight nor for present use alone. Let it be such work as our descendants will thank us for.

—John Ruskin, philanthropist

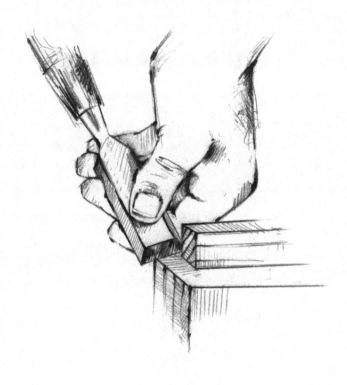

CHAPTER 12

Chiseled

A mortise is basically a square hole cut into one piece of wood, and a tenon is a projection carved into an adjoining piece that allows the two pieces to fit together. Both can be achieved with a hammer and a chisel. Some of the finest woodworking you'll ever see is the result of the meticulous hand of a carpenter chipping away until every cut is as close to perfect as it can be. There's something about turning off the saws and quieting the hum of the dust collection system to sit and work with a chisel. A nice sharp chisel can do the kind of detail work that makes the whole project come together. In chiseling and in life, slow and steady carries the day. You can't finish a marathon in a single step, nor can you carve out a table in one sweep of the chisel. Rather, you stay alive and present to this one fine cut in this one moment—the only one you have for sure.

"Hey, Clint!" a producer said to me over the phone. "Could you bring your tools from the shop and set them up here and just sort of build some stuff on-site?"

The site, it turned out, was the driveway of a local couple, the McNamees. Their home was chosen for the pilot episode. As I would learn, when you're filming an episode for an actual season, the story lines are somewhat structured and the filming schedule is pretty straightforward. But a pilot is different. You throw everything at the wall and see what sticks. Yes, the producers have sketched out a general plan, which you follow, but you also film just about anything else that comes up along the way. You shoot what feels like enough scenes for a feature-length film so there's plenty of footage from which to choose, and in the end, it's boiled down to about forty-six minutes of television, which amounts to an hour-long episode once commercials are added. On day one, everyone is fresh, nervous, excited, and ready to make TV history. But somewhere around the third week, you find yourself in a long, seemingly never-ending grind. Joanna had already been at the pilot house for weeks, working her heart out trying to design this thing, and Chip was there doing his thing as well. Somewhere in the middle of that long grind and right after the house had been demo'd, I got the call from the producer.

"Yeah, sure," I said. I was still a one-man shop, and loading up my table saw, planer, lathe, chop saw, hand tools, and everything else should've sounded like a pain. But to the ten-year-old in me, the kid who once figured out how to move his entire bedroom upstairs from the basement using a bedsheet as a furniture dolly, the producer's request sounded like a challenge I wanted to take on. I loaded everything up, drove down the road, and set up a shop in the driveway.

Those first scenes took only about fifteen minutes to film. "Do you think you can make an island to put here?" Jo asked me as we walked around the kitchen, with the camera crew trailing us.

"Absolutely!" I told her.

"And if we pull some of this antique pine off the walls"— otherwise known as the famous *shiplap*—"can you make a table out of it?" she asked. "Yes, ma'am!" I said. Joanna then added a final item to my to-build list: a vent-a-hood to go over the stove.

At that point, I'd completed a couple dozen tables. I'd even built a few islands. But I'd never made a hood vent cover. I'd seen them, and I'd even installed a few exhaust fans at some of the Habitat houses. But making a wooden enclosure for one that would look pretty and be custom-built to house the fan? Well, it wasn't impossible, but it was one more thing I was just going to have to figure out.

The same was true with the filming itself. We zipped through the first three scenes I was in, with Joanna asking me about the projects I was set to build, and that was it. In my head, I'd envisioned a director occasionally stepping in to say, "Cut! Let's do that again, only this time with a little more energy, okay?" That didn't happen, and it's not because I'm magic on the screen. When the filming ended, I grabbed my tape measure, got over the fact that I'd felt flat and wanted a do-over, and went looking to recruit a couple of guys on the jobsite with carpentry skills. No way was I going to take on the hood cover without help.

The next day, with some reclaimed wood in tow, I pulled up to the driveway of the pilot house. The day before, the guys I'd found helped me put together a basic frame for the hood cover, leaving room for the fan and ductwork. Now, with the cameras rolling, I just needed to make it look great. That turned out to be harder than it seemed. Most of the angles I was trying to cut weren't even possible with the only miter saw I owned, and I had to jerry-rig a contraption to make it work. It was the perfect recipe for an accident. Throw in the stress that comes with being filmed, and you can see why that was such a dangerous move. Thankfully, it didn't cost me a finger. I tried to relax, slow down, and work at my own pace. Over the years, while singing or speaking in front of people, I'd learned to breathe my way through nerves, but when that little red light on the camera flashed on, it changed everything.

That pilot house was never quiet. Production assistants rushed around with clipboards and headsets. A saw was always running.

No one seemed to stop. Amid the busyness, I continued making my pieces, and Jo filmed a few times around my makeshift shop, discussing each of the projects and how she was hoping they'd turn out. Occasionally, as I was minding my own business, a camera operator would walk by, aim the lens at me, and pick up some B-roll (extra footage used to fill in the gaps in an episode and give it a bit more depth). It was exciting and stressful, and everything in between. Each evening as I finished up, I moved the evolving pieces into the garage for storage overnight.

Meanwhile at home, Kelly and I were still on the brink of financial implosion. After the job at Habitat didn't work out, I was seriously thinking about going back into the sales field. The furniture I was building for Jo just wasn't bringing in enough yet to keep us afloat. It felt, once again, like I was going to have to shelve the carpentry work and get back out in the nine-to-five. On one hand, I was all in as I built these projects for Jo and tried to make my impact felt on the show, but would it even register on the Richter scale? On the other hand, I was trying to find a way out of a money situation that felt increasingly uncertain. My world seemed to be simultaneously blossoming and narrowing, and I was reaching for some kind of sure footing. How long could I continue to show up and do work for a show that, frankly, felt like a long shot?

And yet the miracle wasn't lost on me. Just months after meeting a stranger at a gas station, I was making furniture on the set of a TV pilot. It was the last thing I would've imagined doing back when I was in my Houston garage trying to figure out how to make a table out of pallets. In leaving the sales job, I'd signed up for a life that would come with its share of twists and turns. But this twist—playing the go-to carpenter on an HG-freakin'-TV show—had been nowhere on my radar.

As the cameras rolled, I kept working. And of the three items I'd been asked to build, the table was my favorite. It had straight legs and a skirt that wrapped around the legs like the farm style Jo and I had used many times before. I stained the base and painted it white so I could distress it with sandpaper once it was dry. As I rubbed the sandpaper over the legs, it slowly brought out the darker-stained wood underneath. On the top, I applied poly to enhance the beauty of the natural wood. It was rough, and meant for the outdoors, as it would ultimately go under a newly built pergola. I loved it.

In November 2012, filming ended; the pilot was set to air the following May. That December, Kelly and I cradled our sweet Camille for the first time. *Time for me to buckle down*, I thought, gazing down at her adorable tiny face. *Time to get serious about making a buck as a full-time carpenter, with no cameras around.*

*   *   *

In order for a business to grow, you usually need more money and more people. You need other things, of course, but I'll focus on those two. For me, I couldn't pull money out of thin air (let me know if you figure that one out!), but I had a sneaking suspicion that if I could find more help, more business would come my way. In other words, I had to increase my productivity and grow beyond my one-man woodworking operation to establish a sustained enterprise. So I did what any close-to-broke entrepreneur would: I spent more money I didn't have. In March 2013, I invested in hiring someone to help me part-time. That person turned out to be Britt Duke.

Britt and I met during my days volunteering for Habitat, where he still worked at the time I was looking for help. I'd heard from a mutual friend that he wanted to "build stuff" on the side—like maybe some kids' toys. By this time, Kelly and I had started attending church again, and Britt and his wife, Holly, happened to sit in front of us one Sunday.

During the whole service, all I could think about was whether I should say something to him, and if so, what. I didn't want him to think I was attempting to pull him away from Habitat, but I had heard through a friend that he was interested in carpentry, and I needed help. I figured it couldn't hurt to throw out a line. I caught up with him and his wife after the service.

"Hey, Britt and Holly!" I said.

"Hey, Clint," he said. "How's it going over at the shop?" Given that my shop had once been Habitat's cabinet shop, he knew exactly the space I was working with.

"It's good," I said. "Things are coming along. Listen, I was thinking the other day . . . well, a friend actually mentioned you might be looking into building a few things here and there. Do I have that right?"

"Well, I guess," he said. "I mean, it's nothing too serious, but I thought it might be fun."

"Right. Well, look, absolutely no pressure here, and I know you're busy working with Habitat—but I was thinking, if you had any time after work or on the weekends, I could maybe use a hand."

His face lit up. "Really?" he said. And then he added: "Well, actually—and please keep this to yourself for now—I'm considering moving on. I've been there for over ten years and I think it's time for a change. I'm actually looking at another option right now, but if you've got an opportunity, well, I'll listen. Why not?"

We agreed to meet at my shop later that week and talk through the possibilities.

Kelly and I went home and looked over our budget. Even though Kelly probably thought I was crazy—and for good reason, I might add—she once again braved the unknown with me as we sat on the couch and came up with a number that maybe, with such little cash flow, we could scrape together to consistently pay Britt. A few days later, I picked up lunch for us, and right on time, Britt and Holly walked through the door. There I was, seated on a workbench and surrounded by piles of wood and scraps. I greeted them and then dove right in.

"Okay, here's the deal," I began. "You know that I quit my job in Houston to pursue this dream of building furniture, and things have gone all right. I'm not completely overwhelmed with orders, but I hope I will be. I'll be incredibly candid: I can't afford to pay you much. Quite frankly, $750 every two weeks is really all I can do . . ."

Before they could respond, I pressed on, telling them more about our company, what projects I was working on, and of course that little thing called *Fixer Upper*. "I know the money's not much right now," I said, "and quite frankly I can't even guarantee that I'll even have the cash when it is actually time to pay you. But I will promise you this: I'll do everything I can to make sure we make some money, and if this *Fixer Upper* thing goes anywhere, we'll be busier than we can handle. And regardless of it all, this will be a wild ride. I promise you that." That was it, the only pitch I could possibly make. The honest one. He deserved that.

We finished our lunch, looked at some tables around the shop, and talked for a bit more. He had to look into the other opportunity, he told me, and he'd get back to me after that played out. So I waited. And about a week later, he called with news that sent Kelly and me to the moon: "Hey, Clint," he said. "I'm in."

I couldn't believe it. I had my first employee! He gave his notice at Habitat, and a couple of weeks later, right before Easter, he started at the shop. The moment he walked through the door, my cool factor went up. He was a drummer. He wore these awesome dark-rimmed glasses and had a full-on beard. He actually looked like a carpenter. I, on the other hand, had just enough facial hair that I had to shave it every morning to keep from looking like I was in perpetual puberty. I wore these light-colored jeans and ugly T-shirts that Kelly hated. Britt was mellow and witty, and I was loud and goofy. "We should take a selfie to commemorate this first day," he said. Until that moment, I'd never heard of a selfie. He grabbed his phone and snapped the shot. The picture was horrible, but it has become one of my all-time favorites, as has Britt.

On March 29, Good Friday that year and soon after Britt had started, I walked into the shop with my eyes puffy and red. "Oh man," Britt said. "It must be bad." It was: moments before, my mother had called to tell me that my uncle Howard, her eldest brother, had passed away.

Uncle Howard had stood six feet three and was as husky as an NFL lineman. My grandmother used to call him the "Rock of Gibraltar," but not only for his size. He had a strong personality, just like his father; he was opinionated and fiercely loyal. When he was in a room, he commanded your attention just by standing there. At the same time, he could be the most loving person you'd ever meet, with his huge smile and rosy cheeks. A few days before Good Friday, he'd gone into the hospital with a serious infection. Due to major complications, he was gone. Just like that, our family was crushed.

I got in my car and drove all the way to Alabama, where his family lived, so I could go to the funeral and say my good-byes. When I returned, I buckled down in the shop like never before. I was reminded how quickly life can be taken from any of us, and I resolved to do the job right. I wanted every breath, every experience, every moment, however many of them I had left, to matter. I didn't feel pressure. Rather, I finally felt the freedom to relax and really enjoy this whole journey I was on.

That headspace lasted until, two weeks later, I had to deliver my biggest project up to then: an entire bedroom set for a client in Dallas. Britt and I scrounged up some oak and pecan pallets and put all the pieces together. We worked right down to the wire, leaving ourselves just enough time to load up a moving truck and transport the furniture all the way to Dallas, and just as important pick up our paycheck. We were also picking up more wood in Dallas, thanks to a deal we'd made with a local businessman. We had to get on the road, and fast.

But we still had one last thing to do: install the drawer slides. In hindsight, leaving this to the end was a major mistake. They didn't fit. As the clock ticked, Britt and I were feverishly putting the drawer hardware on and then taking it back off to make adjustments. I was stressed, and Britt could tell. If I couldn't make drawers fit on our first big project together, I thought, how could he feel confident in his decision to jump on the Harp train—and by "train," I mean something closer to the one Mickey conducted in Disney's first cartoon than a powerful locomotive. We stripped the screws. We couldn't get anything to work. At one point I let out a frustrated "Aaaaahhhhh, dammit!!" which Britt would later admit almost made him throw up. It felt like the wheels were coming off our bumbling choo-choo.

Settling myself down, I grabbed my chisel and went at it. There were fine little cuts I needed to make in order for the drawers to fit. It was the kind of task that requires you to stand still and work in small motions. This is the hardest work—the kind that, with sweat pouring down my face, I was attempting as I fine-tuned that chest of drawers. It's the work no one will ever see. The little adjustments to make things fit. The quiet, stressful moments where if things don't finally fall into place, you may just tear the whole thing up. This is usually when you want to give up. But you don't. You just keep working that piece till it's right. You keep shaving off little bits till it fits. You keep on telling your kids to say "Thank you" in the hopes that they will one day be contributing members of society.

You keep talking with your spouse, all the while believing that you'll somehow work it out. You keep running. You keep trying. You close the shop door and turn a leg one more time. You move forward. This is the work no one will ever see, but it's the most important work that we can ever do.

Britt and I made it to Dallas in time. Barely.

That whole nerve-racking experience made me remember a woman I'd learned about and admired greatly, the sculptor Augusta Savage. I'm drawn to sculpture. I don't study it, and I'm certainly not an authority on it. I just appreciate the work that goes into it. I love the tools, especially the chisels, and I love the idea that the artist starts out staring at a massive stone, allows the piece to reveal itself, and then tirelessly chips away until the art is born. As I was chiseling away at those drawers that day, trying to birth my own art, I thought about Augusta Savage. An African American artist born in the South in 1892, she grew up in a racist and male-dominated world, yet she carved out a life for herself through sculpting and even founded her own studio in New York City during the Harlem Renaissance.

Her detailed, beautifully cast figures are a powerful reminder for me of the human ability to plow forward in the face of countless obstacles. Rejected from studying at an art institute in Paris because of the color of her skin, Augusta Savage was herself an extraordinary example of fortitude, sculpted by years of struggle. I'd imagine Augusta had days when she wanted to walk away. When she wanted to go inside, turn up the music, sit back with a cold one, and just say, "Forget it." In the spring of 2013, I often had that feeling myself. But I had an employee. I had three kids. I had a savings account with not a single dollar left in it. So I kept chiseling away. I didn't give up. And neither did Britt. Day after day, he showed up at that shop with no idea how everything would work out, or even if he'd be paid (miraculously, he was, though not always on time). And together, as more orders came in and the work slowly picked up, we just kept building furniture the best way we knew how.

*   *   *

May 2013 rolled around, and finally, it was time for the *Fixer Upper* pilot to air. Chip and Joanna invited Kelly and me and Britt and Holly to a local restaurant, Vitek's BBQ, where they were throwing a watch party with all their friends, family, and coworkers. I hadn't seen the final cut of the episode and had no idea what to expect. Would I even be in it? We all hunkered down, grabbed some barbecue, and turned on the show.

The hour-long pilot literally flew by. We all sat there in the restaurant glued to the screens, feeling so proud of Chip and Joanna and our little town. I mean, this was happening in Waco, for crying out loud! We hadn't received this much attention since our town had made headlines back in 1993 with a disastrous showdown between federal law enforcement and a certain cult leader. But this was positive. Waco looked darn good. And, yes, I was on camera for a brief moment, making plans with Joanna for a vent-a-hood. All that filming I'd done in the driveway, all that time I'd spent building the other pieces—none of it made the cut. But I was just thankful I'd made it into the episode.

We learned soon after that the pilot had drawn sky-high ratings. In short, *Fixer Upper* was a hit. Throughout the entire episode, viewership just continued to rise, and the network paid attention. The excitement around town was palpable. No one really knew what would happen next, but you could feel that something big was coming. When the network ordered season 1, Joanna and the production team didn't have to call me, but they did. I was now—officially and yet unofficially—part of the show.

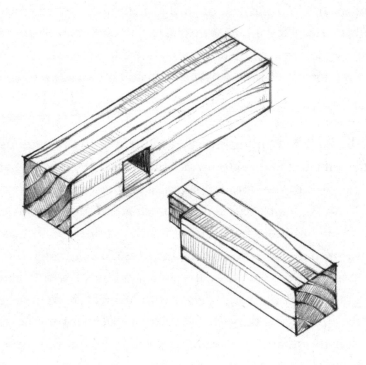

CHAPTER 13

Joinery

If I'm making a jewelry box for my girls, I might join all the sides of the box together using a decorative dovetail joint because it's beautiful, it will last almost forever, and it shows them I cared enough to make them something special. Or if I'm building a table, I'll usually use mortise-and-tenon joinery to attach the legs and skirt. The method is tried and true and tested. Of course with every project, there are surprises, but in the end, if the work is carefully done, everything somehow fits.

A giant house, a high-rise among smaller houses, sits a few blocks away from my shop. A brave young couple bought the place, and it became the project for Chip and Jo's first *Fixer Upper* episode of season 1. "Stop by and say hey!" Joanna told me on the day filming began late in the fall of 2013. I showed up and discovered this thing was totally happening: Hollywood had come to Waco.

When I walked up, Chip was over in the side yard, talking a hundred miles a minute to some lady I figured was one of the folks in charge. I wandered toward them and stood off to the side waiting for an opening in the conversation.

"Hey, Clint, good to see you, buddy!" Chip said. "Let me introduce you to Lauren Alvarez. She and her husband, Steve, are the producers."

She gave me one of those total-body look-overs, her eyes going from my head to my toes and back up again.

"Yeah, okay," she said. "We can work with this."

Lauren would later claim that she was referring to the blue T-shirt I had on, which had our Harp Design Co. logo splashed across my chest. Kelly had worked with a local company to create tees in time for filming, as a way to quickly identify Harp Design Co. to viewers. According to Lauren, "We can work with this" meant the network would be fine with the branding on my tee. But I still like to pretend that she, a glamorous producer from LA, took one look at me and thought, *Oh yeah, this guy looks good*. It was most definitely about the logo on my shirt, but let me have my moment, okay?

Chip told Lauren I was the carpenter guy who could custom-build just about anything for Jo. "We'll call you with a date when you can come and shoot," she told me. And that was that. I got back in my car and drove off, but not before I noticed piles of wood being tossed from the house and into the yard. The demo was under way.

A few days later, I got the call. I showed up at the house, got mic'd, and went inside to find Jo. Inside, Jo stood with Steve while a couple of camera guys and a sound guy were walking around the house, which had been stripped down to the studs.

"You ready to do this, sir?" Steve asked me.

"You bet."

Other than during the pilot, this was the first time I was filming with Jo—and it would be like no other time ever again. With the crew trailing us, we walked around the space that would become the new kitchen and breakfast nook. As Jo explained her renovation plan, she spit out so many ideas that my head was spinning. I think her head was spinning, too. We walked and talked in circles, and the cameras just let us keep going, with no clear end in sight. Jo finally asked if I could make an island for the kitchen. Check. She also wanted a bench for the nook. Double check. The whole walk-through probably lasted only fifteen minutes, but six or seven design brainstorms later, I was exhausted.

I walked outside to catch my breath. I heard a loud bang and looked up. There, on the rooftop, a crew of workers were tossing ten-foot planks of antique shiplap pine from the second story of the house down into a dumpster below.

"Hey, hold on a sec!" I yelled up as I ran closer. One of the guys looked down at me. "Hi, I'm Clint! Can you wait a minute so I can look in there to see what you're throwing away?" He nodded.

I climbed up the side of the dumpster and dove right in. I was right at home. All around me was beautiful wood, and it was all mine, if I could dig it out. And dig I did. I started throwing the wood back out and onto the ground, creating my own pile to haul back to the shop.

"Hey, wait a minute, Clint! Stop!"

I looked up and Steve was running toward the dumpster.

"Hold up there, pal!" he shouted. "Let me get some cameras over here! We gotta get this on film!"

And like that, the dumpster-diving, reclaimed-wood-loving carpenter was born—at least in the TV world. To this day it's how I often get introduced, and when I do, I always think back to my first day of filming for the inaugural season of HGTV's new show, *Fixer Upper*.

*　　*　　*

Kelly and I were committed to keeping Harp Design Co. going despite the challenge that it was. In terms of sleep deprivation, 2013 was proving to be a landmark year: a new baby kept us up around the clock, even as we juggled the growing demands of our three- and five-year-olds. And at the shop, orders were slowly ticking up.

Around town, people were starting to hear about this guy who built furniture from pallets and scrap wood, and who'd appeared on the *Fixer Upper* pilot. Shortly after it aired, a local community college professor asked me to build him some simple bookshelves, which I happily did. He happened to be connected to *Bohemia*, a small local magazine that some of his former students had started. When the editor approached me for an article, I was stoked. Good thing I'd snapped some pics of the hutch and name tag cabinet I'd built for the church in Austin. Those photos were featured in the mag.

When the story came out that fall, Kelly and I really began to feel a shift. Not because the article was widely read, but because our furniture design work had now been committed to print and of course to film, which made it somehow more real. Suddenly, the future of Harp Design Co. wasn't just a dream we talked about while sitting around our kitchen table; other people were now in on the conversation. And with all the local chatter about the new HGTV pilot and forthcoming home renovation series set in Waco, how cool was it that Kelly and I could say we were part of it? It changed our own perspective on what we were doing with the business. It helped even us see it as established.

It hadn't, however, altered our financial reality. Though I'd been cast as Jo's go-to carpenter, that role did not come with a network contract or payment. It was true that we were getting more orders, but unfortunately, we still didn't have quite enough. Every two weeks when it was time to pay Britt, it was a miracle that I actually did. On multiple occasions in those days, the power in our shop was turned off. That's because I'd wait till the very last second before the bill was due to pay it, hoping we'd have the money by then. Often, we came up short. The next morning, I'd arrive at the shop to discover that the utility company had left us in the dark, and I'd quickly call and put the balance on my credit card, ensuring that the lights would be turned back on an hour or so later.

Usually on that same day, Kelly would send me a text from the grocery store: "Clint, the debit card was denied again. They're putting our food in the store's walk-in freezer. Will you please come by later and figure it out?" That evening, I'd show up at the grocery store with a different credit card, hoping this one would go through so I could bail our groceries out of jail. But no matter how deep the hole financially, we did do one thing right: we did not touch the mutual fund Kelly's grandmother had left her.

Things got so scary at one point that I had to pull Britt aside for the one conversation I'd prayed I'd never have to have with him. "Britt, I hate to say this," I said as we sat in the shop's carport, eating our lunch, "but we may need to look for jobs. Don't send out your résumé yet—just get it updated. I really don't want to go get another job, but it's bad, man. I will say this, though: there's also a good chance we hang on. And maybe one day, we'll have a Christmas party with a dozen or so other employees, and we'll tell this story. We'll talk about how it was just you and me in this shop, thinking this whole thing might not work, and how close we got to shutting off the lights for good."

Six months later, as that watershed year drew to a close, I grilled some sausages on the grate we'd place over a burn barrel behind the shop. Over our lunch together, I handed him gift certificates for two to a movie and a restaurant (a gift card is arguably one of Britt's love languages). I also gave him a battery-powered drill and driver set (not for personal use, of course . . . it was definitely for the shop. But still, it was a gift. Sort of. We put his name on it). It was the first Harp Design Co. holiday bonus ever to be given out. We'd made it through the year. With sheer determination, Britt and Kelly and I had somehow figured out a way to cobble together enough work to keep everything going. We weren't out of the woods, but we also weren't underwater. We'd survived. And what better way to celebrate than by purchasing a crack house?

*   *   *

Chip and Joanna filmed just about every day, but I only showed up on set when Jo called me in for a project. Of the first season's twelve episodes, I built something in about five or six of them. I spent most of my time back at the shop with Britt, making tables and just trying to keep the lights on. One afternoon at the end of 2013, again over lunch in the carport and not long after I'd given Britt that "bonus," I started dreaming out loud.

"What if Kelly and I bought this shop one day?" I said. "We've always wanted a storefront, and I bet we could turn this carport into one. I mean, I know it's a neighborhood in transition, but it could be a diamond in the rough!"

Britt, who obviously has a risk-taking streak as well, was all in. Then I put another idea on the table.

"What about that place over there?" I said, pointing toward the former drug den next door (which thankfully, in the year following my move to the shop, had become vacant). "Maybe one day we can turn that into a rental or something."

It was hard to picture. The two-story white farmhouse was a total eyesore. The front siding was adorned with a few bullet holes, and it had major heaps of trash scattered around its yard. It was a dump.

"You know, Clint," Britt continued, "I was talking to a guy who builds houses in this area, and he mentioned that the couple who owns that place might want to sell it. Apparently, they're asking fifteen thousand for it."

That's when my interest perked up. I didn't have that kind of money. *But wait—just fifteen thousand?* That got me thinking. "Let's go walk around it, Britt." Seconds later, I tugged on the front door of the abandoned building. It was locked tight. "Come back here, Clint!" Britt called out. He'd discovered that the back window was open.

Being a bit OCD and germ-phobic, I thought I might never again touch Britt when I found him crawling through the kitchen window and into what turned out to be the kitchen sink. He scrambled to his feet and then let me in through the back door. The place was beyond a disaster. And it smelled as horrible as it looked. Scattered on the floor were beer bottles and trash and papers and clothes and anything else you can imagine. Furniture was strewn around the place, with couch cushions slashed and mattresses leaning up against the walls. Every room, every closet, every bathroom—all of it was filled with more garbage than was humanly possible. And for some reason, it seemed perfect.

I told Kelly about it. She was hesitant. As you know, my wife is usually the one pulling me into a house, going, "Hey, let's get this place and fix it up!" and I'm the one who's usually like, "Uhhhh . . . I don't know." I can't blame her for being reluctant. The place was a hellhole, and our funds were nonexistent. "But it's right next to the shop," I said as I presented my case. "We could clean it up and turn it into something great." In my view, it was the ultimate reclamation project.

"Where would we get the fifteen thousand?" Kelly pressed, and we filed the idea away as a future possibility and got on with our lives. But Britt and I would occasionally let ourselves in through the back door when we just wanted to dream a little. Bill, the husband of the woman who owned the place, even stopped by our shop one day and talked about wanting to sell it. He was a loud-talking guy with colorful stories and salty language, and he was as persistent as he was persuasive. The $15,000 price still made me salivate, but Kelly and I weren't willing to touch our last-resort mutual fund for it.

One morning about a week before Christmas, Joanna and the *Fixer Upper* crew showed up at my shop to shoot a design scene with me. Since I had no agreement locked in with the network, I wanted to make sure that every experience they had working with me was a good one. As the film team rolled up, so did Bill. He came rumbling down the back alley in his old truck just as the crew pulled into the front of the shop to set up in the lot where we usually parked. It was like they were on a collision course toward each other. I tried to turn Bill around, but I was too late. He turned the corner into the lot and got out.

"Hey, Clint, how's it going?" he yelled, as boisterously as always.

"Yeah, you know, it's going okay, but it's not a good time right now," I said. "I've got a bunch of stuff going on, and some people coming to the shop, soooo . . ."

"Sure, no problem," he said. "I totally understand." But he of course kept right on talking. "I'll tell you what," he continued, "here's what I came to offer you. If you buy my house by Christmas, I'll sell it to you for ten thousand."

Not what I expected. "Bill, wow," I said, glancing over my shoulder to be sure the crew wasn't calling for me. "Um, yes. I will take that deal. I mean, I think I will. I need to talk to my wife and figure out the money. But okay."

I raced back into the shop and filmed with Jo, but I have no memory of what we did that day. I just recall a clock ticking in my head the whole time. As soon as we got done, I called Kelly and told her about the offer.

"I don't know, Clint," she said. "I'm not sure I want to use our mutual fund for that."

"Let me talk to Joe Nesbitt at the bank," I suggested. "I'm sure he'll laugh me out of the room, but you never know." That idea really made Kelly feel better, as she was pretty sure no banker would lend us the money for another house.

I sped to the bank. And there was Joe, sitting behind his desk as if he'd been waiting for me.

"Clint, do it," he said after I'd told him about the unbeatable offer. "I'll get you the funds and we'll get this deal done. I'll call the title company and get it set up. You just go tell the guy you want the house. Go find a Realtor you can pay yourself, and make sure you get the right paperwork signed and whatnot. You got this, buddy!"

That was on a Monday. On Tuesday, we lined up a Realtor to help us close on this house, which we planned to renovate ourselves and turn into a rental in order to help clean up the area around our shop. And on Thursday, we closed on the deal. But it was what happened on Wednesday that was the real game-changer.

Kelly was in the parking lot at Target, wrapping up one of her usual runs with the kids to pick up a few items for a new design project she was getting ready to start.

"Hey, Kelly!" called out Joanna.

"Oh, hey!" Kelly said. "How are you? And how's filming?"

"It's great," Joanna told her. "It's a ton of work, but going really well. I'm just happy to have a free moment to get some shopping done. How are you guys?"

"It's insane right now, with Clint trying to build as much furniture as he can with Britt," she said. "But it's good. This week has really been nuts. You know that ugly house right next to Clint's shop?"

Joanna nodded. "It's pretty awful."

"Well, we're buying it."

Joanna's eyes widened. "Kelly," she said, "we have to do that house for the show!"

"Wait, what?"

"Seriously, Kelly, let's do it for the show! We need more houses. It'll be great!"

"Oh wow, yeah, I really don't know," said Kelly. "I mean, I would love for you to be a part of redoing our house, but we were planning to do all the work ourselves, especially since we're on a very limited budget. But let me talk to Clint."

"Let *me* talk to Clint," Joanna exclaimed, laughing. "We're doing this!"

At home, just as Kelly was telling me about her parking lot meeting with Joanna, the phone rang.

"Hey, Jo!" I answered.

"Clint, you're doing it," she said. "Come on. This will be amazing. It'll practically cement you as the carpenter on the show, and the whole episode will be about you and your wife and your family and your business. Come on!"

How could I argue? She made a lot of good points. We were in.

*　　*　　*

Christmas came and went, and we began counting down to when we could rip into the new project. Chip and Jo were traveling on business, and the house couldn't be touched until they returned on January 14. Kelly and I used those first two weeks of 2014 to map out a plan. Joe at the bank had helped us land a $100,000 construction loan. That may sound like a lot of money, and it is, but every square inch of that hovel, from the rooftop to the floorboards, would have to be ripped apart, cleaned up, and made new again. It was no small task, and it came with no small price tag, so we needed to use our loan wisely. It was decided that for the show, the producers would focus only on those areas that would appear on TV: the front entry, the living room and dining area, the kitchen, and the exterior, which left us with the whole rest of the house to fix up on our own. Bottom line: We'd be far more involved in our own project than the typical *Fixer Upper* homeowner.

The day arrived, the cameras showed up, and the demo crew got after it. When I tell you that house was a mess, that is the biggest understatement I've made yet. All told, two and a half full-size dumpsters were used to haul off just the trash from inside the house. And that didn't include the nasty cabinets, toilets, sinks, and everything else that would have to be removed. Sick.

Every inch of drywall was removed. All the shiplap was pulled down from the walls, particularly since I wanted to be sure every rat's nest and God knows what else was eradicated. Every inch of copper electrical wire—the ones that hadn't already been torn out and sold for drugs—was pulled out and thrown away. All the porn in the attic, tossed. The pipes, most of the floor, the ceiling—you name it—gone. I wanted nothing left, because I didn't want to harbor any part of the sadness that had once lived in that house. Every window and every door would be replaced. New water and electrical lines were run. Duct work for new air conditioning was installed. Even the roof was stripped.

As eager as Kelly and I were to see the progress and ultimate final outcome, we had to step away so we would be surprised by what Chip and Joanna delivered. Back at the shop, I got busy on the projects I needed to have built in time for the big reveal. It didn't help that I got the flu in the middle of it all, which knocked me out for a week—seven days I didn't have to spare. I bounced back and hit my work schedule hard. I constructed an island for the kitchen, a vent-a-hood (my second, following the one I'd made for the pilot), and a front door for the house. "Can you go over to the house and do some measurements for me?" I'd ask Britt, who of course agreed.

On the night before the mid-March reveal, I worked with Britt and Jacob—a local college kid and restless adventurer who'd randomly stopped by the shop a few weeks earlier to see if he could volunteer—late into the night, planing down wood and cutting out tongues-and-grooves so we could clamp it all up and have it dry in time to make TV magic. We were there till four in the morning.

I finally lay my head down around 4:45 a.m.—and lifted it right back up at 6:30 a.m. so I could sand the front door before the 8:00 a.m. reveal. I showed up at 7:00 a.m. with my eyes still half-shut, and at around 7:45, I filmed a scene with Chip taking the door from the shop so it could be installed at the house. I then quickly changed my clothes, and fifteen minutes later I was standing in the street with Kelly behind a giant movable billboard with a picture of our house in its original state staring right back at us. On the other side of that billboard was John Alexander, my old friend and the former director at Habitat, who seemed to always show up when I most needed him. He was feverishly hanging the just-delivered front door, making sure it would look good enough for television once that billboard parted.

At last the billboard was pulled aside. I will always remember the look in Kelly's eyes. She was as stunned as she was relieved at the gorgeous two-story that stood before us. As we embraced, everything we'd hoped and imagined for this house clicked into place.

Next, Chip and Joanna gave us the TV tour of the house, and as we walked and talked and *ooh*ed and *ahh*ed at how perfect it all was, I thought of my granddad Martin. I couldn't help but tear up. A few months earlier, his health had begun to deteriorate, and his mind was fading. Seeing our new home with the wooden pieces I'd contributed to it would've made him so proud. In the span of just eight weeks, a house that looked like it should've been condemned and torn down was standing pristine and rejuvenated. From the chaos, a treasure had been created. Somehow, as my mom liked to say, it had all dovetailed together. Standing there with Chip and Jo, we were just so thankful for the work they'd done and for the way they'd invited us into this journey with them.

When the filming was almost complete, we all took a seat on the couches while the crew reset for one last scene. Chip and Jo and Kelly all eventually got up to look at something and stretch their legs, and I was left just sitting there with Rog, a camera guy. The next thing I heard was Rog yelling, "Clint's falling asleep! Let's get this show wrapped up before we lose him for good!" I popped back up, everyone else filed back in, and we shot our final scene and called it a day.

In April, exactly four weeks after filming that reveal, Kelly and I moved into our new house with our kids and all our belongings in tow. In that month's time, she and I had taken turns away from work and caring for our children to stay up overnight painting and caulking and tiling and doing whatever was needed to finish the rest of the house. Kelly's mom, Debbie, moved to Waco from Kerrville and worked on the house with her during the evenings and also helped with the business and the kids. We couldn't have done it without her. During the day, Britt and Jacob did whatever was needed to get it done. It was the most exhausting time of our lives up to then. What we didn't know was that just around the corner, as the *Fixer Upper* phenomenon heated up, things were about to get even crazier.

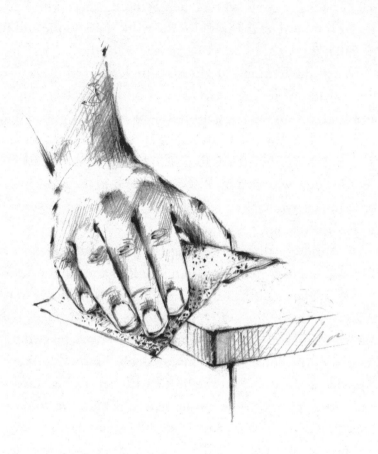

CHAPTER 14

Final Touches

When attaching a tabletop to its base, I like to use z-shaped clips that allow for seasonal movement. As the table absorbs humidity or loses moisture, depending on the surrounding atmosphere, the clips let the top move on its base ever so slightly, making the finished piece less likely to bow or crack. Now that there's a fully assembled table in front of you, it's time to go over it one last time. Just as you wipe your kid's face and flatten down that rogue hair in the back before he or she walks into school, you take one more swipe with a piece of sandpaper or one more decisive cut with the blade of a chisel before sending that table off to be finished. Apply a coat of stain only to find out you didn't remove all the glue, and you'll have to sand everything down and start over—cumbersome and time-consuming, to say the least. So I walk around the table with a sander and a chisel and make all my last-minute touch-ups. I might dull the corners a bit for a more worn look, or I'll make all the edges nice and crisp for a modern look. I take my time and look at the piece from all angles, because this is my last chance to apply the subtle refinements that will have a big impact on the look of the finished table.

"Clint, what's the longest table we've ever made together?" Joanna had just walked into my shop with this question. I thought for a moment. "Sixteen feet," I told her. "For that house on the river last season."

"Awesome," she said. "Let's make one longer."

"Longer than sixteen feet?" I said.

"Yes, I'm thinking seventeen."

"Done."

The third season of *Fixer Upper* was under way, and Chip and Jo were hard at work on what would become one of viewers' best-loved episodes, "The Barndominium," about a horse barn turned condominium in the countryside suburb of Lacy Lakeview. It was now the summer of 2015, and we were practically old hands at this TV thing. After a certain crack house transformation in season 1, I worked on a variety of projects for the show, including a rickety hundred-year-old Craftsman that Chip nicknamed "Three Little Pigs," a down-on-its-luck 1960s ranch house, and a so-called "Shingle Shack" near Lake Waco. I'd been called on to build everything from farm and craft tables to fireplace mantels, cubbyhole hallway units, and barstools. I had not a spare moment—and plenty of great memories.

Like during the second season, when Chip and Jo gave a "modern coastal" look to a house called the "Faceless Bunker." For the table Jo asked me to build, she wanted me to tie in wood and metal and then make benches in the waterfall style—which essentially means that the bench top looks like one very long piece of wood that has been bent at both ends at a perfect right angle so the grain is continuous throughout the whole piece. Previously, I'd mixed gas pipe with wood in making tables and shelving units. But as far as a giant table base welded together and grinded down smooth and finished with a satin black finish, which was what Jo was requesting? I'd never tried that, nor had I attempted a waterfall edge. But of course, I agreed to take it all on.

The guys and I came up with a plan for the waterfall benches: we'd create a perfectly flat core using three-quarter-inch maple plywood and then wrap that in the actual wood we made the table from, which was antique pine. This allowed us to create a three-inch-thick board. About 18 inches from both ends we made a perfect miter cut and then rejoined that cutoff to the piece we'd just sawed it from at a right angle. Voilà—waterfall edge. For the base that would compliment our massive wooden top, we stepped out into a bit of the unknown. Fortunately, I had Jacob on my team. Our skinny wunderkind from Houston was curious about almost everything, and that curiosity had once led him to a welding machine back in high school. We had a metal guy down the street provide us with some square metal posts, I bought Jacob some cheap metal-cutting tools, and he brought his welder to the shop. He got right to work and knocked it out of the park. When it was done, it was a thing of beauty. He ground his welds and painted it a satin black. I'm so proud of that piece because it just shows what you can do when you work with people and put your heads together and get creative and use everything you have.

Another one of my season 2 faves? The so-called "Tire Swing House" makeover for the Gulley family. In that episode, Jo asked me to take some old flooring ripped out of the back of some eighteen-wheelers and transform it into an island top. I went over and shot the scene with Jo. I pulled up and found J. D. Scott, older brother to Jonathan and Drew Scott of *Property Brothers*. Even as early as the second season, it was apparent this thing was turning into something more than just a little show about some house flippers in Waco.

As soon as I walked in, Jo and I started filming the design scene. We talked for a while as we walked around the place, and I found some eight-foot sections of laminated-edge grain maple flooring resting on the floor. You had to manhandle one just to move it two feet over! Gluing all these together to make one giant seven-foot-square island top was not only going to be a bear, but it was also going to create a piece that would weigh as much as a small car. My mind was racing with the logistics. The cameras needed to reset, so we took a quick break. Steve, the producer and by now also my friend, pulled me aside and said, "Hey, take this rag and this bottle of water and say, 'Hey, Jo! Take a look at this . . . it's like magic.' And then wipe the wet rag over the dirty lumber and show her how pretty it's going to be when you finish it!" It was genius. And also completely obvious, or at least it should have been. And in a normal situation without a camera in my face and that red light shining, maybe I would've thought to do that. But with everything swirling around, I was literally just caught up with the details of making such a large piece. But that's why the producers are there, and Steve and his wife, Lauren, were both great at that. Making TV really is a team effort.

Chip and Jo hadn't just connected with viewers as they wowed the world with their renovations. They'd also helped turn our sleepy little town into a hot destination. With the cameras rolling, they began the conversion of a massive grain barn in the heart of downtown Waco into Magnolia Market at the Silos, an enormous store, bakery, and garden that sits on two and a half acres and features all things Magnolia. Business boomed. Tourists from all over the country were descending in droves. Viewers had embraced Jo's warm smile and "shiplap" lexicon, Chip's humor and antics, and the couple's on-the-farm life with their "kiddos." They were a real, relatable, all-American family. Throw in Jo's undeniable skill for incredible design, and you can see why the ratings were through the roof. Viewers loved the show, and it seemed they couldn't get enough. It was an exciting time.

But for all its entertainment, what made the show so special, in my humble opinion, was its authenticity. The show is a genuine reflection of Chip and Jo's lives off-camera, and ours too. Jo really is a self-taught interior and exterior designer who sold home goods for years before a producer ran across a blog post about her and she hit it big. Chip really was buying real estate around Waco, fixing it up, and flipping it with Jo. And Kelly and I really did travel a winding yellow brick road—from a basement kitchen in Paris to a cement-cracked garage in Dallas, through three kids and multiple maxed-out credit cards—to launch Harp Design Co. around our kitchen table. None of that is made up, and I've always loved the fact that the show is so organic. For over a decade, we'd all been scratching, clawing, wandering, and hoping to create the life we'd always imagined we could have.

And now there we were.

Not long after Jo asked me to build the Barndominium's seventeen-foot-long table, I'd hit the carpenter's jackpot. Just down the street from my shop, an older man who'd crafted furniture for over fifty years was moving on. He and a crew had built cabinets and tables and even eight feet of a spiral staircase that was never finished, back in the seventies. When I walked into the man's shop for a visit, the staircase was still there, as if someone had just moments earlier set it aside to work on something else. I was there because I'd heard the power company was planning to buy out his business and others around it so they could run power lines through the area.

"Hi, I'm Clint," I said. "I've got a woodshop up the street. I heard you were selling a bunch of your tools and whatnot."

"Yes, sir, that's the story," he told me. "I don't do too much building anymore, so I'm just selling everything off. Take a look around and let me know what you like!"

Tools were scattered all over the place. Much of the good stuff had already been claimed. Just as I started to think this had been a wasted trip, I looked up. Above me were a couple dozen wooden trusses that spanned the width of the shop. All of it had been nicely preserved. My heartbeat sped up.

"Um, excuse me, sir," I said. "This may sound crazy, but what about the roof?"

"The roof?" he said, raising his brows.

"Yes, sir," I said. "I'm wondering what you're going to do with the roof. Is this place going to get torn down?"

"I believe so," he said. "That's the plan. But . . . you want the roof?"

"Well, yeah, if you don't mind," I told him. "I'd love it. If I bring a crew in here to tear this thing down, would you be okay with that?"

"I don't see why not," he said. "Let me clear my stuff out of here and then you can have it. Just be careful!"

When Jo and the *Fixer Upper* crew asked me to build that seventeen-footer, I of course was so quick to say yes, even though I didn't have the foggiest idea where the wood for it would come from. But by this point I was finally catching onto the reality that if I really needed it, the wood would be there. And there it was in the form of an old carpenter's roof, just waiting for me to come along. Plentiful and right on time.

By the end of filming, Chip and Jo had pulled off their usual miracle. The result was a contemporary two-story with Old World charm, complete with a LEGO wall, a children's play space, and beautiful hardwood floors. I completed the enormous table, and it was so long that I had to borrow a trailer just to haul it over to the house. When the episode aired a few months later, there sat my art piece, crafted entirely from reclaimed pine, gracing the Barndominium's stately dining hall on the first floor. Up to eighteen people could be seated around that grand seventeen-footer, courtesy of an old carpenter who provided the wood and a younger carpenter who, only three years earlier, had built his very first farm table.

By the time I created the table for the Barndominium episode, it had really started to hit us just how different things were going to be for us. Our family went on vacation to the beach with our best friends, Jen and Patrick. It had been our annual tradition. On our way to the beach that year, with the *Fixer Upper* phenomenon well under way, we stopped at a restaurant for lunch. Without blinking an eye, a lady walked right up to our table and said, "Oh my gosh, you're Clint, the carpenter from *Fixer Upper*! I love that show and I just feel like I know you!" And as our presence on social media grew, we started to see ourselves getting tagged by people who had happened to see us somewhere and just snapped a pic. It was pretty clear from that point on that things were changing. Our lives. The city of Waco itself. My family's sense of normalcy. It was both an exhilaration and an adjustment, all at once.

* * *

In all but the first season of *Fixer Upper*, I appeared in over half the episodes. Each time I was on the show, I'd spend around an hour filming the design scene with Jo, and maybe another half hour to an hour when I delivered the item to the house. Meanwhile, Chip and Jo and the crew would be sprinting to keep up with an impossible filming schedule. Not everything always went true to plan. Several times, the polyurethane on a table was still wet as we delivered it to Jo on camera. And on one occasion, Jo wasn't exactly thrilled with the look of a table base I'd finished with blue milk paint at the request of one of her design assistants, and she had one of her guys repaint the base in white. I'll never forget walking in with the table in my hands and the cameras rolling and immediately knowing she didn't like it. I still to this day wish I had said in the scene, "You hate it, don't you?" Instead I just rolled with it and waited till the cameras turned off to ask her thoughts. I was right, and it would've made great TV. But all in all, the *Fixer Upper* experiment had gotten off to an insanely good start. We'd put our whole hearts into every project, and it seemed to be working out.

During the second season, I had turned some candlesticks with a white distressed finish, and even gave Jo, on camera, a crash course in turning. Those bad boys became an overnight sensation. The next thing I knew, I was underneath a pile of orders for two thousand candlesticks, which we sold through our online shop (apologies to all those we frustrated with our tardiness as I tried to keep up with the sudden demand). Thankfully, we had some more staff by then. In 2014, as Harp Design Co. had become more visible, I'd expanded my team: Jacob and Marco joined Britt and me in the shop. At the end of that year, Kelly and I were euphoric because our company had at last generated real revenue. We'd brought in just north of $40,000. Though we were at last making a little money, I honestly still don't know how we were managing to pay three employees, feed a family of five, and keep our lights on. Yet somehow, we did.

The show had given us an awesome platform, but the real work of building our business happened offscreen. With cameos in multiple episodes, Harp Design Co. continued to grow and we found ourselves adjusting to instant exposure. As we grew, the projects I'd do for Jo and the show would become a smaller percentage of our overall business, which had to happen if we were to survive. We had to stand on our own two feet. From cutting boards and candlesticks to farm tables and benches—HDC was custom-crafting hundreds of pieces in a year. On top of that, Kelly and I were juggling the needs of three kids and finishing the renovation of our home, which, following the on-air overhaul, took another two years to complete.

As the company grew, Kelly and I finally revisited the dream of turning the shop's carport into a storefront where tourists and locals alike could purchase our handmade furniture, as well as Kelly's designs and curated home goods. The guys and I worked to transform the open-sided carport into an attractive enclosed space. But when it came to actually getting the store up and going, it was my wife who picked up the ball and ran with it. When she was done, she'd created a masterpiece. I couldn't wait to invite our first customers over. The dream was real.

Next, we built a pole barn for wood storage, and a finishing shed—which, if at all possible, needs to be a separate space so that sawdust doesn't get into the varnish. We also bought and renovated a warehouse space, and carved out an office for the people who'd eventually join our team. That crew, as of this writing, is twenty-five strong. Our incomparable staff would grow from Britt, Jacob, and Marco to include Demi, Kristin, Andrew, and John, along with many others who would help us make this thing happen. And of course my mother-in-law, Debbie, who lived down the street from us and did just about any and everything, plus some. Many nights she'd be up late in that cold, damp warehouse, packing boxes to ship out the next morning. She also worked in the storefront, which we opened to customers in 2014. She quietly did more for us than we could ever repay.

As thrilling as it was to be part of the *Fixer Upper* phenomenon, the dream for Kelly and me had always been exactly what we found ourselves doing when the cameras weren't rolling: building a homegrown business from the floorboards up with the help of an unbelievably great team; daring to wander off the beaten path and blaze a trail of our own; and working with my hands the way my granddad had taught me at the Roost. That dream was finally becoming real.

Then in the midst of our excitement about the strides we were making came a sobering reminder of life's fragility. Brooke, my uncle Howard's daughter—the fun-loving, no-nonsense cousin I'd shared so many good times with at the Roost, and who had supported and celebrated me through every twist and turn of our *Fixer Upper* journey—was in a tragic accident. Driving to work one morning, she was hit by a motorist who'd suffered a heart attack, lost control of the steering wheel, and swerved across the median into my cousin's lane. In an instant, she was gone. With my heart in shreds, I made the same cross-country trek to Alabama to attend her memorial service at the same funeral home where her father had been laid to rest. Even with all the filming and fun stuff we were doing, losing Brooke made it all feel a little less exciting. She was one of my biggest cheerleaders, and once she was gone, it took me a while to find joy in it all once again.

* * *

Lindsey, an HGTV exec who essentially managed *Fixer Upper* and developed other new shows decided one day to reach out to me. I'd heard of her before and had gotten to know her through social media, and I liked her vibe: hilarious, hardworking, creative. I was in the parking lot between our house and the shop when she called.

"Clint, I'd like to produce some online content with you, maybe some two- or three-minute videos documenting the process of you building something for Jo and the show. Would you be up for it?"

"No-brainer, Lindsey," I told her. "Just tell me what to do."

"Great!" she said. And then right before she hung up came this stunner: "Just be awesome and don't suck. You never know, it might turn into your own show one day."

I ran into the house and told Kelly. We couldn't believe it. Who knew, when I was sweating it out in my makeshift garage sweat lodge years before, that we'd end up here? We were pumped. From day one, we'd been delivering tables to Joanna and the network based on a smile, a nod, and a handshake, but now maybe an actual contract was in our future.

When some of our friends and *Fixer Upper* crewmates heard about my new opportunity, they were like, "Nice work, Ty Pennington!" Being compared to the famous carpenter from *Trading Spaces* and *Extreme Makeover: Home Edition*? Yeah, right. Give me a break. But there was no doubt I hoped there might be a smidgen of truth to their predictions. You don't bust your tail to launch a home design company and then pray it languishes in obscurity. This was potentially huge, and I intended to make the most of it. Besides that, back in our early days of marriage when Kelly and I would watch every episode of *Trading Spaces*, Ty had been my favorite.

But things tend to take a while in TV land, and this project was no exception. The year rolled on and my team and I knocked out more projects for *Fixer Upper*. Finally, several months later, we began shooting our webisodes. I had a crew of one: a local freelance camera guy and an all-around creative dude, Zack. On the first day of filming, he showed up at the shop with the camera the production company had sent to him. That was it.

"Hey, I'm Zack," he said.

"Awesome, come on in," I said, shaking his hand. "You ready to do this?"

"You bet, man! It'll be fun. Oh, and by the way, I figured it would be kind of loud in here, so I brought my own lapel mic. That'll help us a bit."

We were seriously on our own. This wasn't even a low-budget B movie we were making. This was going to be more like a home video of my garage time. The network execs weren't about to throw the bank at a simple three-minute web video. There was no script. No director. A handheld camera and a borrowed mic. But hey, it was my shot, and I was going to take it. I hadn't had everything I needed when I set out on this path, so why would this be any different?

Over the next four weeks, Zack would come by the shop and capture me and the guys as we plugged away at our projects. It was November by then, and freakin' cold for Waco, with temps dropping lower and lower. We'd shoot for fifteen minutes and then walk out to the burn barrel and warm our hands to bring them back to life. I asked my friend Steve, the producer on the first two seasons of *Fixer Upper*, if he'd come by and give us some direction. He was kind enough to oblige one morning, free of charge. He watched us film a scene and then broke in: "Okay, great job, Clint, but here's the deal. Say everything you just said in that three-minute span again, and see if you can do it in, like, fifteen seconds." I did my best to be as concise as Steve suggested, but let's just say brevity is not my forte.

The entire series was shot through the dead of winter. We finally wrapped and sent it all to the production company. A few weeks later, my phone rang.

"Hey, Clint, it's Lindsey at the network."

"Hi, Lindsey," I said, excited to hear her feedback. "So what did you think?"

She drew in a breath. "Those were the worst videos I've ever seen," she said. "Literally, they were awful." She was just articulating what I'd feared in my gut. Even to me, the webisodes had felt hammy and staged. I'd done exactly what she'd told me not to do: I'd sucked. Not everything you do works out, folks, but sometimes the heavens smile down on you. Lindsey had decided she would give me another shot.

Two months later, Zack returned to the shop, this time with Jason, a freelance producer, at his side. With Jason's help, we sorted out our whole webisode saga and sent four videos to the network. This time, the footage included Kelly and my kids and more of our life around our shop. And this time, the webisodes were enough to carry us to the next exciting step: a few months later, the network asked us to create a sizzle reel. *Whoa!*

I knew we were in good hands when *Fixer Upper*'s production company, High Noon, sent Michael, one of their best camera-men, longtime sound guy David from Chip and Jo's crew, and their top-notch producer Glenna, who produced *Fixer Upper* and managed to make me look like I halfway knew what I was doing every time I appeared on the show. It was in large part because of her work that my brief on-camera appearances felt integral to the episode. "Hey, Glenna!" I greeted her enthusiastically. "Kelly and I have already lined up a family so we can mock up a scene where we build furniture for them. We can then transform their space around that piece, and . . ."

"About that idea," she said. "So there's been a bit of a curveball."

"What's that?"

"Your show is getting turned into an outdoor show."

I gave her a blank stare. "You mean, like, I'll be building furniture outside?"

"No," she said, laughing. "Like you'll be transforming someone's outdoor space."

Right.

I enjoy looking at good landscaping as much as anyone else when it's done well, but it's just not something I'm personally good at. Our friends Steve and Lauren, the producers, had always told us, "Hey, if they ask you to do a show about butterflies, just do a show about butterflies. Take what you're given, and you'll eventually get to do that thing you want to do." With their advice in mind, Kelly and I moved forward, but reluctantly. An outdoor show just felt so inauthentic to us. We knew the network was trying to give us what they felt was our best shot at succeeding, because, let's face it, they weren't too sure about a show highlighting a carpenter and his wife as they built tables from their more-than-modest shop. It wasn't until a cameraman pulled us aside that we bought into the whole thing.

"Listen, you guys," he said, "everybody knows you're not land-scapers. Who cares? We're not going to shoot it like you're experts. We're going to capture who you really are. You're risk-takers. You're two people who aren't afraid to try something new and test the boundaries and limits of your skills. You've proved that you can make furniture, and you still will. But the key here is to shoot you as you are, trying something new. Just go with it. Take the skills you've learned in the shop and apply them outdoors."

Bingo.

That day's footage was probably the best we ever shot. The cameraman's words helped me to let go of my reservations and just sink into the process, because he'd been exactly right—taking risks was what I'd been doing my whole life. And together, Kelly and I had tons of experience in figuring things out and making a tough situation work.

The sizzle reel ended up being a true-to-life snapshot of our family, our business, and our teamwork as husband and wife and fellow entrepreneurs. We were elated to learn the reel had landed us a pilot on the DIY Network, an HGTV affiliate that was also owned by Scripps. The show was tentatively titled *Against the Grain*, and in the fall of 2015, Kelly and I inched farther into unknown territory.

We were given two backyards to transform, each with a pool that had to be demo'd and fencing that needed replacing. One backyard was a normal suburban size; the other was more than a half acre. In twelve days of filming, not only did we do all the demo work . . . we had sprinklers installed, laid fresh sod, had retaining walls built, constructed decks in both yards, and remodeled a barn which Kelly designed from top to bottom. We also built an outdoor movie screen, a double-decker kids' playhouse, and a pergola with a ten-foot island made from old reclaimed fence planks. On the last day, every single person on our team, as well as all the camera crew, was either staining a deck, laying sod, or both. It was insane. Exhausted and worn thin, we finished, feeling incredibly proud of what we'd pulled off.

Unfortunately, few people would ever see it. "Clint, the network loves the episode," a producer told me. "Really and truly, you and Kelly did great. But the overall thought was 'Let's make this show more about the shop and what they do as a company.'"

And just like that, our nearly two weeks of stress and perspiration tumbled to the cutting room floor. But all was not lost. The network decided to splice together some footage from our backyard projects with video from our earlier webisodes, plus a few of my *Fixer Upper* scenes. Voilà! A pilot was born. It pushed us on to the next step—and that, for us, has always been enough.

CHAPTER 15

A Strong Finish

As I wipe the last coat of finishing oil on a table I've just made, I feel like I'm saying good-bye to a friend. I really do keep all the memories that came along with the construction of that table. I think about the conversations and jokes that were shared around that table, even when it was still in the form of unvarnished planks, pieces strewn across my shop floor. I love it when a tabletop, one that was previously laid out in its roughest state, finally emerges from the sander. In that moment, I see what the piece was meant to be all along, with its grains and colors and beauty all working together. Adding one final coat of oil gives that grain a wet reflection. In it, I see the entire journey—the one I've just completed and the one my creation will now begin.

When we were filming the *Against the Grain* pilot, I was helping coach my daughter Holland's soccer team. I vowed not to miss games if I was in town, which was less and less frequent as I traveled to speak at home shows and bring in income to reinvest in our business. Back in 2011 when I put in my two weeks' notice at the sales job, the last thing I thought I'd be doing was getting booked for speaking gigs or making a living as a carpenter in front of a camera. Hell, I was insecure about whether I could even build furniture. Doing it on TV for the world to see wasn't even on my radar.

Nor was being a model. (Stop laughing . . . I'll explain.) That's right: Clint Harp, the onetime kid with a head three times too big for his body, whose fashion choices were driven by whatever I could piece together from the secondhand items in a black trash bag, got a call from my agent (another thing I never imagined I'd have) about a possible endorsement deal. This was in 2016, in the middle of filming the fourth season of *Fixer Upper.*

"Hey, Clint," he told me, "we have a cool opportunity for you, and it's probably not what you're thinking. Are you ready for it?"

"Sure! Give it to me!"

He laughed. "Okay. You wear watches, right?"

"Every day without fail," I said.

"Well, Citizen Watch called, and they'd like you to represent them."

A single thought reeled through my head: *Why?*

"They'd love to partner with someone who is also actively working with renewable resources," he explained. "They also like the idea of teaming up with someone who's recognizable, but who still seems like a normal guy. You in?"

So stinkin' fun and random! "I mean, sure," I told him. I was more than willing to wear some watches and take some pics.

When it was time to fly to New York City to meet the Citizen team at their new flagship Times Square space and take part in a photo shoot, I had zero idea what to expect. When I landed, a driver was waiting for me at baggage claim. That was new. I was taken to the InterContinental hotel just off Times Square. As I walked into the lobby, I saw a crowd of folks gathered on my right. The next thing you know, they were greeting Jill Biden! It was a wild scene. That night as I dozed off, imagining what this photo shoot would be like, I kept thinking, *These people do know I'm seriously just a bucktoothed kid from Atlanta, and kind of an idiot, right?* It was unbelievable to me that I was even in Manhattan.

The next morning I woke up early, got myself ready, and walked outside to meet my driver. A giant black SUV whisked me away and dropped me off at a modern-looking building. Very industrial. In my head, I was showing up to something like an Olan Mills studio from 1984 to meet a photographer with a point-and-shoot camera. The reality was way cooler. I walked inside and approached a young greeter at the reception desk.

"Hi, I'm here to take some pictures with Citizen?" I couldn't bring myself to say, "Hey, I'm the model." That sounded stupid to me. I mean, please.

"Yep, up the ramp over there," said the receptionist.

At the top of the ramp I saw about thirty impeccably dressed people, whisking around, sipping coffee, and looking all New York–ish. I scanned the room in search of someone with the point-and-shoot around his or her neck. No such person. I finally went up to someone and said, "Hey, I'm Clint, and I'm supposed to take some pictures with Citizen today?" It was more like a question than a statement of fact.

"Oh, hi!" said the woman, setting down her coffee. "So glad you're here. Right this way, follow me."

When I was twelve, my mom used to ask me to sing solos in front of her friends, and for whatever reason, that made me want to run and hide. But put me in front of two hundred or two thousand people instead of just one or two, and I feel good. I don't get very nervous. In fact, I tend to come alive. Given that I come from a line of artists, singers, and comedians, that makes sense. But when I followed this complete stranger into an adjacent room and found people milling about everywhere, assistants running around, and incredibly sophisticated photo and video equipment being set up—well, I got jittery.

"Kelly, I think I might throw up." That was the text I shot off to my wife. Next thing I knew, I was standing inside what looked to me like a quintessential New York City loft studio, painted in pure white and complete with an exposed-brick accent wall, the kind of space you might see in a Jennifer Aniston movie or Beyoncé video. I felt way out of my league. But when the Citizen folks crowded around and introduced themselves, I found myself put at ease by how down to earth and fun they all were, even when they told me that Eli Manning and Kelly Clarkson had been their previous spokespeople. *Then why the heck did you call me?* I wondered. I learned I'd be shooting a TV commercial that day, print ads the second day, and social media on the final one. Soon after, I was sitting in a chair as a director told me, "Just follow my lead and you'll do fine." The lights were blindingly bright and the only person I could see clearly was the director, who sat three feet in front of me the whole time. Behind him were all the decision-makers who needed to like what they saw. Between each take, I could make out the shadows of those people, leaning in and whispering to one another. I was totally convinced they were saying, "Hey, call Eli back right now. Or just any football player. Get me an athlete! Who is this fool?" The director picked up on my insecurity and walked up to me. "Hey, so far I'm hearing a lot that 'This guy looks like Daniel Craig,' so that's good," he said. Not gonna lie: However untrue that was—um, very—it still felt great.

Oddly enough for me though, it was in the hair-and-makeup chair, where I was given that light dusting actors and models get, that I really settled down. The makeup artist practically fell out of her seat when I walked in. "Oh my goodness!" she excitedly said. "You're Clint from *Fixer Upper*! My husband and I love that show.

Oh my gosh! We're trying to buy and fix up a house right now, and you guys down in Waco, you're an inspiration."

For me, hearing that the work I'm part of might inspire someone is one of the single greatest joys of life. It's the best compliment, and I don't take it for granted. As I sec it, we're all traveling around on this giant ball called Earth together, figuring things out as we go. We need to see each other forge ahead and go for broke. It's the fuel that pushes us forward. It did my nerves good to sit in that chair and be recognized for all I've ever really wanted to be—a guy doing his best to create a life that matters. And if I got to have my face plastered on a giant LED screen in Times Square right above Citizen's flagship store? Well, that was just the frosting on the cake—or in my case, the varnish on the tabletop.

* * *

After renovating and living in our *Fixer Upper* treasure from season 1, in 2016, Kelly and I had to make the tough decision to move again and turn what had become known as the Harp House into a short-term rental through Airbnb. We absolutely loved that house. But as Waco started to become a tourist attraction, more and more fans were filling the city. Privacy was becoming a challenge. When you're trying to take a nap on Father's Day and someone knocks on your front door and asks to take a picture with you, or when you're shooting hoops with your son and a stranger pops his or her head over the fence, or even wanders onto the court, it's probably time to set out in search of new pastures.

Don't get me wrong: I love it that so many people are so passionate about *Fixer Upper*. Without the unbelievable fans, the show would never have been the sensation it became. I get that viewers feel connected to the people on the show and want to say hello. I think that's really cool. But I'm also a husband and father who, first and foremost, has to think about the impact that kind of spotlight might have on my kids in particular.

As Kelly and I agonized over what to do, we realized that while the Harp House didn't work for our family's needs, it actually would be an amazing spot for groups of guests. We had once dreamed of owning a bed-and-breakfast and creating a place where families and friends could spend time together. Could we actually provide that to other people, here in Waco? A vision was realized. With Harp House having room for up to twelve people, we had to use every resource we could muster to furnish the place. Somehow we scraped up enough to complete the house. Kelly worked around the clock and made that house shine.

In the end, turning the Harp House into a rental has given others the chance to enjoy the place as much as we once did. To be honest, ever since we bought the $10,000 teardown next door to our shop, I felt like the house was never mine to keep, anyway. It was meant to be shared. So we ended up buying another major fixer-upper home across town, renovated it from top to bottom, and found peace for our family once again.

Around the time we moved into the new house, Kelly and I learned that we'd been offered a second chance at our own show. We ended up making a new pilot called *Wood Work*, and shortly after airing we were picked up for a first season. The concept for the show felt a lot more like us than that previous backyard-makeover blitzkrieg. This time around, we'd be doing what we do best: breathing new life into family homes by handcrafting furniture and even designing spaces around the pieces. So for three months in the fall of 2017, we filmed the full first season of the show. It aired in May of 2018 on the DIY network. But if my turn on *Fixer Upper* has taught me nothing else, it's taught me this:

you don't actually have a successful show until every episode of a season has aired. You don't dare exhale until it's over. And in the meantime, as you're sketching out future episodes and dreaming of what could happen down the line, you do your best to follow Lindsey's advice: Don't suck.

While filming *Wood Work*, my guys and I had a lot of carpentry firsts. None of us had ever built a Murphy bed, a Ping-Pong table, or an entire giant entertainment center out of construction-grade materials found on jobsites. But we did it. And we all brought our different skills to each new project and figured it out. Ratings or no ratings, we were all so stinkin' proud of each piece on that show. So was Kelly. She had designed every space we had ever lived in, and even a few for friends and clients, but never on TV before. Over six episodes, she stepped up and designed amazing furniture and spaces that played perfectly with the work we were doing in the shop. To those who tuned in, the finished product will look like a completed room, but to Kelly and me, each completed design will be a reflection of all the people and hands that made them happen. Kelly and I and our whole team made the whole thing come to life. And that's my favorite part. I'll see Britt finishing beams till the late hours and Andrew running back to the shop to turn an extra leg. Or Kristin staying by Kelly's side to help hang a curtain or a shelf or paint or just doing whatever it took to get it done. I'll see my wife putting herself out there, with her art and skill on display for all to see. It's a hard job, and I've got the best team to do it with.

By the time you read this, our first full season will have aired. However it all turns out, shooting the show was a wonderful and insane ride, one of the craziest my family has had up to now. We shot an episode in Arlington, which is about a hundred miles north of Waco. For that show, we installed a triple-decker bunk bed and made a solid ash custom Ping-Pong table and completely gave the homeowners' space new life. But what you won't see on the episode is how Kelly and I had to step to the back of a moving truck to settle an argument over something so small and stupid that I can't even recall exactly what it was. It wasn't about the pieces we were building or the location of the shelves. At the heart, it was about figuring out how two opinionated entrepreneurs who are always pushing for the best can work together on an intensely challenging project without driving each other nuts. Truth is, I'm most of the problem. For crying out loud, I'm the guy who, during year one of marriage, brought my wife to tears in a grocery store aisle over a stick of butter. I have a hard time letting things go.

Kelly, whose early life had its own share of pain and confusion, has sometimes felt the same, which is why I find it incredibly comical that we would decide to start a company together and work side by side every day. And yet I wouldn't want to walk this road with anyone else. I'm a different and better person because of my wife. And we've made something great together. A home. A family. A life. A love. A business. And even though none of it has been easy, it's been the best and most enjoyable ride of our lives.

I don't know what our show will look like in the end, but every episode is sure to be a thirty-minute snapshot of what can happen if you fight like hell for the people you love and the work you believe in. Ultimately, *Wood Work* is the story of two kids who grew each other up and, along the way, tried to make something beautiful with a band of friends. During twelve weeks of filming, we put all our passions, our hopes, our fears, and our dreams out on the table. We sweated. We cried. We fought. We laughed. And we just about wore ourselves into the ground so that we could finish strong. Whether or not the show finds its own passionate audience in the DIY universe, I can promise you one thing: it will be real.

*   *   *

As we started our family's new chapter, another one came to a close. Even as we were shooting *Wood Work*, my team and I continued banging together furniture for Joanna all throughout *Fixer Upper*'s fifth season. But halfway through, Chip and Jo posted a heartfelt video announcing that season of *Fixer Upper* would be their last. Fans were stunned. Kelly and I knew it wouldn't last forever, but we were surprised as well. In the end, the Gaineses were bowing out when they wanted to and on their own terms, and for the reasons that were most important to them—and that's probably something that needs to be seen more than any episode. Whether Chip and Joanna are renovating houses on the air, or they're off exploring other ventures, they will always be a couple of dreamers and doers, and I love that about them.

Wherever my own path leads next, I'll always carry with me fond memories from my time on *Fixer Upper*, the highs and lows, and those stressful yet exhilarating days when I barely had time to put the final touches on a table before it made its on-air debut. And of course, I'll forever be grateful for the way viewers connected with Chip and Jo, as well as with me, the carpenter; Jimmy Don, the metal designer; and Shorty, the faithful right-hand man to Chip.

Back in season 4, Jo and the crew came by the shop one day and filmed a design scene in which she asked me to build a pair of console tables for the entryway of a house out in the country. That episode will always be one of my favorites. It's such a great example of our teamwork. Jo threw out a design idea, and I contributed my own ideas about how we could build it, and together we came up with something. In this case, I knew I had some thick old slabs of wood out back that we had salvaged from a burn pile. With the cameras rolling, Jo followed me out to our wood barn and I dug through and found the pieces I thought might be perfect for the job.

"Jo, look at these," I said, lifting a heavy block of weathered wood. "I could take these and turn a couple of pedestals, leave it all raw. I think it would rock."

"Yep, that's it," Jo said. "Go for it. I love it."

And that was that. No script. No plan. Just making a design happen on the fly. That's how we did it on the show. It's also how we did it in our lives.

Throughout the filming of *Fixer Upper*, I was asked to build benches, beds, swings, candlesticks, chests of drawers, and of course tables. Some rectangular tables, some square, some with pedestals, some round, some painted, and some stained, and a few incredibly long. Each time I filmed a delivery scene, I'd wait outside of the *Fixer Upper* house, feeling incredibly proud of the work I'd completed with my team back at the shop. Until my very last delivery, that is. Five seasons of crafting high-quality furniture, and my final project was a plywood corn hole set. Corn hole is a simple game, usually played outdoors, during which a couple of people toss beanbags at an elevated ramp with a hole in it, trying to get the bag in the hole. It's great fun, and I actually toss a mean game of corn hole myself.

But even so, building a corn hole set for my last project was a bit anticlimactic. But all that went out the window when I learned that the homeowner was a US Marine. With so many in my family in the service, I've grown up incredibly grateful for their sacrifice. I was only making a corn hole set, but I wanted to make it special. To spice up the design, we inlaid teak down at the bottom and had a local company, Hole in the Roof, engrave the Marines logo in the right-hand corner. It looked amazing, and Jo loved it. When I delivered it, we even played a round, which I'm pretty sure I won, or at least I hope I did, as I think I had talked some trash about my skills. Once we finished, the producer announced, "And that's a wrap for Clint Harp on *Fixer Upper*!" And just like that, an entire era of my life came to an end—in a corn hole.

CHAPTER 16

Around This Table

When I'm done with a table and sending it off to its new home, I'm so happy knowing that family, friends, or strangers will gather around a piece I built. That table will tell their stories and hold their memories. Arguments will be had at that table, love will grow, and laughter will ensue. Breakfast, lunch, and dinner will be served and enjoyed, and buried deep in the table's grain will be the recollection of those meals and the time spent together. Within the fiber of the wood will be family secrets and the kinds of conversations that only true friends share. The table will hold up under the weight of deep pain and intense emotion. Its surface will forever bear the oily marks and elbow grease of those who've lingered there. And it will gladly absorb the carvings of a young boy who might leave his loving mark as a reminder that here, he sat. Here, he dreamed. And here, around this table, he began the journey.

I have wanted to write a book for many years, which is why it's funny that an opportunity I never even imagined—being on TV—came first. In fact, as I look back on these forty years of my life, just about nothing turned out exactly as I thought it would. I play a strange game with myself sometimes: I think about all the possible outcomes of a given situation and predict how it will unfold. I love the game, because I'm never right. No matter how many times I

227

play out a scenario in my head, there are still other possibilities out there. Now, if life is going to be just one big surprise after another, why not veer off the beaten path and invent our own journey? At a young age, amid the unpredictability of my childhood, I decided that's how I'd live. I'd find my own way, and what I didn't know, I'd figure out. What I didn't have, I would work around. What I didn't understand, I would learn. I'd become an apprentice to life and its grand adventures, staying open to the potential in each moment and learning from master teachers along the way.

One of my first master teachers was my granddad Martin. I used to sit at the edge of his jobsites, gazing on as he tore down, built up, and constructed new houses to carve out a livelihood for his family. As the years went on, it became clear to me that there were great chunks of my granddad's life that he'd like to take another crack at, events and relationships he wished he could do over. He never said those words, but his actions and demeanor during his later years showed me that. In his own ways he was teaching me not to make the same mistakes he had.

"I really know how to just walk away from something, don't I?" Granddad Martin once reflected as we strolled through his cluttered hand-built barn, which housed an endless collection of tools and unfinished projects. There were times like that one in the spring of 2005 when he let me in. In that old wooden barn, he cracked open the door a bit, and I could see what haunted him. I could see that he was disappointed and sad, not so much about the state of that barn, but about the possibilities and people he'd let slip away. I could see he felt the pain over some of the choices he made, and I could feel him hoping I'd choose a different path.

A few weeks later he gave me a challenge.

"Clint," he asked me, "have you ever taken a hand planer and done the work with your own muscles to make a rough piece of lumber just right?"

"No, Granddad, I haven't."

"Well, you need to," he told me. "You need to make a table using all the old tools. The way the old-timers used to do it. Take your time. And do it right the first time so you don't have to go back and do it again. Make it last forever."

For the longest time, I thought he was talking about furniture. And of course, in some ways, he was. But whether he or I knew it in that moment, building instructions weren't what he was passing down to me. He wasn't handing down the timeless craft of classic joinery, or reminding me that wood could be bent, twisted, and shaped by hand tools just as well as it could be cut and sanded by machines. He was telling me to do my life right. He was telling me to see him, his life, and what he had left unfinished, and do better.

My grandfather was a builder. He was also a man on whom I'd trained my eyes from an early age, and I kept him in my sight until the day he died at age ninety-three. He knew I was watching. And for all that he decided not to care about along his own journey, he decided to care about me. He made sure I knew how important it was not simply to get a job done, but to excel at it, to be thorough and meticulous and passionate about whatever I was creating. A man I loved who had gotten life wrong on many counts was passing along the art of getting it right.

I accepted his torch. And as I've poured my heart into learning his craft, I've picked up a few techniques of my own. I've honed my woodworking skills late into the night and in the early hours before dawn. I've stood over my lathe making countless table legs, candlesticks, pedestals, and bowls. In the heat of the Texas sun, I've sweated from every pore while making tongue-and-groove joints and chiseling out the tightest mortises I could. Alone in my shop, or alongside my crew, I've battled with my inexperience as I've tried to figure out the next challenge. I've also sat alongside millions and watched myself on television, looking like a master craftsman and knowing I'm anything but.

What I am is a journeyman. A dreamer. A kid who once sat at the base of a tree and imagined what was possible. A guy who now stands at the foot of the mountain trying to claw my way to the top, knowing there's another peak right around the corner. These days, I'm okay with landing in a field of unknowns and being required once again to figure things out. I'm okay with the uncertainty and unknowns of life, both in carpentry and in my walk of faith. I'm not the guy who once left for Europe, thinking I had all the spiritual answers for the world. Not even close.

I'm walking through this world not in search of a trail to follow, but in recognition that the trail is waiting for me to blaze. It is up to me to truly be me. And if Kelly and I love each other well; if we love our children with all our heart; if we live our lives with love for anyone who crosses our path; and if we try to become the best versions of ourselves, day by day—that will be the greatest work of our lives. If we achieve that, maybe our kids will grow up and do the same and one day pass that on to their children.

Once I figured all this out, the Bible stories and scripture verses of my youth began to make so much more sense. The pieces slipped together. If God truly does want me, the person He created, to be a reflection of His love, creativity and power, then doing the work I was put here to do is the best way for me to accomplish that. And for me, right now, part of that work is in a carpentry shop, my face covered in sawdust, my tools in hand, and all my security blankets tossed aside. And some of that work is also sharing my story, whether through public speaking, writing a book, or making a show. And I share it not because I think it's the most amazing story ever, but rather because I hope that my experiences might push you forward in yours. We all have something to give, and in my case, that's a story of a boy who grew up to make tables—a place where all people can come together and find common ground in a world that is increasingly divided.

*   *   *

Wood and glue. Simple ingredients, but incredibly sturdy and effective. Use them right and everything will fit together and stay that way for a long time. Using these tried-and-tested methods always makes me feel more connected to the master woodworkers who passed down their hard-won wisdom and techniques. When I can tell the new owner of a piece I've built that their table or hutch or vent-a-hood was put together using wood and glue, with not a single nail anywhere, for me that is where carpentry and artistry intersect. But while craft is super important, woodworking is also about function. Serendipitously, right before I started building furniture full-time, I caught a documentary about charter schools in New York City, and it highlighted a young, hardworking single mom in Manhattan who spent her days doing everything she could to care for her daughter. At night, they came home to a small apartment, which was completely empty except for a short stepladder and two mattresses on the floor. When it was time to eat dinner, the mother served her daughter mac and cheese. The little girl placed the plate on the top rung of the stepladder, sat on the bottom rung, and slipped her legs through as she settled down to her meal.

That single image stayed with me. It eventually helped tip the scales. And I wanted to see as many families sitting around a table as possible, because it's around a table that we learn and grow and dream and find love and work through doubt, and gather with others for the most important moments of our lives. The tabletops, the skirts, the legs beneath—the basic wooden pieces shaped by carpenters for centuries and held together by classic joinery and some glue—provide more than just a place to sit. They give us a space in which to craft our lives.

*   *   *

I'd been sitting at a table in Baylor's Armstrong Browning Library for three months straight, writing this book in a room that looked like it was from the set of *Downton Abbey*. One day toward the end I looked around and noticed a verse by the English writer and poet Robert Browning engraved on the base of a bookcase which read, "As the runner snatched the torch from runner still." It struck me that I hadn't noticed this before and I decided to look up the poem from which it was from. The lines were from his famous poem "Paracelsus," which celebrated the life of a master alchemist. I was further struck by these lines: *But you have link'd to this, your enterprize, an arbitrary and most perplexing scheme, of seeing it in strange and untried paths.*

Strange and untried paths. Those words resonated like a gong. The verse itself seemed to frame my story—my adventure. I hoped that as I pursued my "arbitrary and most perplexing scheme," I'd continue to enjoy the process of learning, of figuring out how to strum a guitar and use a lathe, and meet the endless number of unknown experiences that would no doubt come my way. I hoped to never feel like I knew so much that I didn't have to keep searching for answers, and I hoped never to forget that life is a constant surprise.

I've been a carpenter on one TV show, and by the time you read this, knock on wood, I will have been on a second one. But that is just a part of my story. As thankful as I am for the chance to connect with all those who tune in, I certainly didn't quit my six-figure sales job to become a television personality. I walked away because I wanted a life that fulfilled me. I walked away because I wanted to make a contribution that would last long after I'm gone. With Kelly's blessing, I traded an existence that was comfortable for the terrifying unknown, because I hoped our kids would one day look back and see what's possible when we go for our dreams. In the end, my life has been about dusting off old passions, living without a safety net, and leaving a mark on the path for others to follow. And that's more than the point of my journey. As I see it, it's the purpose of everyone's.

I've enjoyed writing this book even if the process was much harder than I could've ever imagined. Now I'm going back to the shop to build something. Probably another table. A table where all are invited, all are welcomed, and all are encouraged to be the only thing they should be—the truest and most beautiful version of themselves possible.

Acknowledgments

I've long thought that gratitude might just be the key to life. If you can find something or someone to be thankful for, in even the harshest of situations, you can probably make it through. When it comes to the scores of people who've come alongside me, both on my path to the present moment and in the writing of this book, I don't quite know where to begin, but here goes.

To my beloved wife, Kelly: Thank you for believing in me. Thank you for being my partner in this insane journey, and most of all, thank you for choosing me. I am the lucky one. I could only be so fortunate as to be sitting on a porch with you one day when we're in our nineties, looking back on a life well lived.

To Hudson, Holland, and Camille: Being your dad has brought me the kind of joy I'll never quite be able to describe to you. Each one of you makes me smile every day just by your sheer existence. As you grow up, I hope you know your mother and I want nothing more than to see you be who you were made to be.

To Mollie Glick, my literary agent: You are amazing. Thanks to you and Matt Horowitz and all those at CAA who helped bring this book to life. I truly appreciate your belief in this project, as well as the hard work you put in so I could get my shot.

To Michelle Burford, my coach and cowriter: I couldn't have done this book without you. How you stumbled into my path is a miracle, and I'm so thankful for everything you poured into this story. Maybe one day we can put on tight red sweatpants and paint the town.

To my awesome editor, Matthew Benjamin, and the whole team at Touchstone and Simon & Schuster: Thank you for taking a chance on me and my story.

To Darrah Gooden, a dear friend to Kelly and me: Thank you for lending your unreal artistic talent to the illustrations in this book.

To Robert Sebree, you have photographed seemingly every musician, actor, and artist there is over the last however many decades . . . and then lucky me got to step in front of your lens. Thank you for your amazing work making me look presentable for the jacket of this book. BBQ on me.

To my parents (all four of them!): Thank you for loving me. Thank you for raising me. And thank you for giving me the life I've had. It truly is the reason I'm here today, and your love and support have shaped me into who I am. Mom, thank you for teaching me to laugh, and love, and hang on till it hurts. And Dad, thank you for teaching me how to make people laugh and for putting a ball in my hands.

To my siblings (full, half, adopted . . . whatever!), Bonnie (and Mike!), Becky, Suzanne (and Mitch!), Ben, and Miracle: I am lucky to have you in my life. Thank you for going for your dreams and being the wonderful and beautiful people you are.

To my uncles and aunts and cousins and nephews and nieces: Thank you for the incredible parts you've played in my life.

To my mother-in-law, Debbie (Mimi!): I just don't know what we'd do without you. Through every journey Kelly and I have taken in our married life you have played a pivotal role. You are irreplaceable. There are hours of work where you poured out your own blood, sweat, and tears which no one will ever see. Without them we wouldn't be here. Thank you hardly feels like enough.

ACKNOWLEDGMENTS

To my father-in-law, Bob, and his wife . . . thank you for your love and wisdom and support as Kelly and I continue to jump out into the unknown and take on whatever comes our way.

To Johnna and Jonty: If things don't work out like we hope they do, can Kelly and the kids and I just come live at Wood Farm with you guys? I'll sand as many boards as you need, Jonts!

To Paul: You were right. Things really did take on a life of their own. I now find myself covered in sawdust at the end of the day, and I hope you're somewhere on a park bench covered in birds.

To Chip and Jo: Well, I'm just really glad I needed gas that day in 2012—and that you did, too! Thank you for asking me to build those first tables when I had very little to show for, and for making me a part of *Fixer Upper* when you didn't have to. It's hard to put in words, truly, but I'm forever grateful. Whenever you need a table, Jo, I'm there.

To everyone at the old Scripps, which is now Discovery, Inc.: Thank you for the chance you give me to do what I do in front of a camera.

To our team at High Noon Entertainment: Thank you for every second you've pored over film, making me, Kelly, and our team look good. And please keep making me look like I know what I'm doing . . . I need all the help I can get!

To Britt Duke: You'll never know, amigo. I can't even begin to thank you for stepping out like you did to become part of our crazy venture when you had every reason to run for the hills. You don't work for me . . . I get to work with you, and I'm so thankful I do.

To John Alexander: Thank you for being one of the most genuinely kind and honest people I've ever known. Throughout my journey in Waco, you've always been a part of the story, and I'm so thankful.

To Joe Nesbitt: Are you crazy?! Thank you for loaning me money and believing in me even after I showed up in your office covered in

237

sawdust and left it all scattered on your desk and your floor. I'm a mess, but somehow you saw deeper. I'm grateful for you, my friend.

To my whole family at Harp Design Co.: You guys are truly the best. Whether you work with us now, or you've worked with us in the past, you've played a huge part in getting us where we are today, and you make HDC what it actually is. Kelly and I are so thankful.

To my friends, mentors, teachers, former pastors and ministers, and second families: Thank you for pouring into my life. Thank you for being there for me when I felt like I was lost. Thank you for loving me when you didn't have to.

Thank you to singers and songwriters and artists everywhere: As I wrote this book, I was never without my headphones and a powerful song. So many musicians have inspired me through their work, and it has always pushed me forward. I would need a whole 'nother book to lay out all your names and the work you created that has inspired so many.

To all those I've bumped up against on my own personal journey: Thank you, because you've been a part of my story, whether or not you know it.

And to the people at the beautiful Armstrong Browning Library on the campus of Baylor University, thank you for letting me take up residence there for months as I typed out over eighty thousand words in the creation of this book.

To Grandmom Camille and Granddad Donald: Kelly and I took a picture when we worked on our first house, just like the two of you did so many years ago. I miss you both so much.

To Grandmom Ann: When I was still a youngster, you pointed me in a direction that would push me forward and eventually make me the man I am. Thank you. You were among the strongest women I've ever known.

ACKNOWLEDGMENTS

To Granddad Verner: I've tried my best to do it right the first time, just like you told me to. I'm not sure I've always succeeded, but I've tried. If you could see some of the things I've built, I hope you'd also see yourself deep in the grains of my creations. You weren't perfect, but you didn't have to be. You were what I needed, when I needed it. You put tools in my hands and grit in my heart so I could find my way farther down the road. You old buzzard—thank you.

About the Author

Clint Harp can be found regularly on HGTV's hit show *Fixer Upper* as the dumpster-diving, reclaimed wood–loving carpenter and furniture artisan. He and his wife, Kelly, own and operate their business, Harp Design Co., and star in the new DIY Network show *Wood Work*. The Harp family lives in Waco, Texas. *Handcrafted* is Clint's first book.